*Restoring the
Virginia Governor's House*

Restoring the Virginia Governor's House
Preserving a Historic Home for a New Century

Roxane Gatling Gilmore

Foreword
Colin G. Campbell and Nancy N. Campbell

Copyright © 2012

ALL RIGHTS RESERVED
Printed in the United States of America

Published by The Dietz Press
Petersburg, Virginia
www.dietzpress.com

No part of this publication may be reproduced, stored in a retrieval system or transmitted
in any form or by any means, electronic, mechanical, photocopying, recording
or otherwise, without the prior written permission of the publisher.

ISBN: 978-0-87517-140-1
Library of Congress Control Number: 2011938818

Table of Contents

Foreword vii

Introduction ix

Chapter 1   Alexander Parris Designs a Governor's House 1

Chapter 2   The Governor's House Changes with Time 15

Chapter 3   Defining the Project and Assembling the Team 23

Chapter 4   Where We Started–Governor Tyler Would Have Felt At Home 31

Chapter 5   Using Technology to Gather Historical Data 41

Chapter 6   The Hallway, a Janus 47

Chapter 7   The 1813 Rooms 57

Chapter 8   The Ballroom 67

Chapter 9   The Dining Room and Breakfast Room 75

Chapter 10   The First Family's Living Quarters 81

Chapter 11	The Basement	87
Chapter 12	The Governor's House Welcomes Everyone	97
Chapter 13	Expanding the Project to the Whole Compound	103

Postscript 111

Appendix 113

Notes 123

Glossary 127

Bibliography 131

Index 133

Foreword

Only great care preserves a great home.
 And great care requires a great heart.
 Not to mention a sure and steely sense of purpose.
 First Lady Roxane Gilmore provided all that and more to preserve and sustain Virginia's historic Governor's House and tells about it in this delightful and informed account.
 By embracing Virginia's legacy of historic preservation, Mrs. Gilmore worked within an admirable and durable tradition. In telling her story of the restoration—a restoration carried out under her leadership—Mrs. Gilmore makes valuable points about the inevitable balances that must be made between what it takes protect an important property, while adapting it to existing and foreseeable future needs.
 For one thing—and this should come as no surprise for anyone who has launched themselves into the rigors of preservation—it takes a lot of patience. It also requires an abundance of commitment, diligence and very importantly, restraint—meaning a readiness to embrace the physician's creed and, first, do no harm.
 Guided by these values, Mrs. Gilmore took on the challenging assignment of creating a 21st-century home for Virginia's governors and their families while respecting the landmark building's role as a space that physically embraces Virginia's public continuity and does so with distinctive style and gracious hospitality.
 In this volume, Mrs. Gilmore introduces us to the "nuts and bolts" of restoration, to the difficult decisions that had to be made in the face of incomplete evidence about one or another design element and to

what seemed at times as seemingly intractable obstacles to be overcome. She emphasizes the teamwork essential to the process, the detailed and exacting research, the design options and the implementation of complex plans.

Archaeologists, architects, historians, conservators and trades were all, of necessity, in the mix. In a time when historic restoration work has made considerable advances, it was critical to be attuned to current preservation standards, to be aware of the latest methodologies and to take advantage of the latest technology. Mrs. Gilmore understood this well, provided the essential leadership and diligently sought out talented men and women to get the job done right.

Like most official government residences, the Virginia Governor's House must simultaneously provide public space for near-constant use, while also affording the governor and his family a place to live that mirrors "normal" as closely as possible. So, in the process of restoring the historic first-floor public rooms and improved the security and building systems, the $7 million project also expanded the second floor family residence, even making the entire structure wheelchair accessible.

Not surprisingly, there were some discoveries along the way, as the reconstruction work uncovered features of the building's historic fabric—some of which had not been seen in nearly two centuries. Previously concealed construction features and decorative ornamentation was carefully documented using the latest photographic techniques and expert commentary. All excavation, demolition and new construction received the same methodical, careful approach.

As well it should have. The Virginia Governor's House is singular. Built in 1813, it is the oldest continuously occupied executive mansion in the nation and basks in the shadow of the magnificent State Capitol designed by Thomas Jefferson.

While other states were inclined to move their chief executives into homes in different settings that were neither historically significant nor easily accessible to the public, Virginia held fast to the notion that the first site—in Historic Capitol Square—was the best site for the Governor's family to reside.

Characterized by restrained elegance, the house represents a locus of pride for the citizens of the Commonwealth and a physical link to its past. It helps tell the story of Virginia, an especially important role at a time when as a people we are not nearly as aware of our antecedents as we need to be to be effective citizens. History tethers Virginians and guides them well.

This was a demanding project, to be sure. First Lady Roxane Gilmore and her team provided a great service to the Commonwealth by leaving Virginia with a Governor's House which has not only stood the test of time but is now in a condition to serve its special role for years to come.

For those who care about historic preservation and for those intrepid souls who just might want to make their own contribution to restoration and preservation, this book is an invaluable guide and inspiration.

Colin G. Campbell
President
Colonial Williamsburg Foundation

Nancy N. Campbell
Chair Emeriti
National Trust for Historic Preservation

Introduction

As Jim and I first approached the stately Corinthian-columned porch of the Virginia Governor's House after his inauguration as Virginia's 68th Governor, I could almost hear the echo of its former occupants reverberating throughout the circular drive: the tinkle of champagne bottles smashing against the corner wall as young Gay Montague practiced to Christen the Battleship Virginia in 1906; shouts of "Fire! Fire!" as flames from a burning Christmas tree engulfed the Ballroom; sobs of mourners in February 1993 filing through to pay tribute to Arthur Ashe as one of Virginia's favorite sons lay in state. These are but a few of the many sounds, both tragic and joyous, that have filled the Governor's House in the 200 years it has been the home to Virginia's governors and their families. It was to these sounds that the Gilmore family began to add our own echoes on the cold January afternoon in 1998 when we first moved into the residence in the northeast corner of Capitol Square in downtown Richmond.

Yet many of the sounds we added during our time at the Governor's House were unlike those of most other families. On our arrival we found leaky air-handlers, sagging floors, and questionable plumbing and wiring. A multitude of problems had beset this old home and were threatening its continued use as the residence for Virginia's governors. And so the rasp of saws, the pounding of hammers and the rhythmic beep of backing machinery were the sounds we brought to Capitol Square during the summer and fall of 1999 as we undertook the major project to preserve the then 187-year old structure.

After the restoration was completed, I began writing about the project, seated at a small computer in the newly restored family library in what I was still calling the Executive Mansion. Much of what I was writing down was what I was telling tours that were going daily through the house about its history and about the scope of the restoration. I hoped the house docents didn't think me intrusive when I would begin telling people what we had learned about the house along the way. I loved to hear from the visitors what they wanted to know, and their questions often sent me off to learn even more about the house and its history.

Over time these notes turned into various versions of a book that many encouraged me to complete. This final version has gone from those early tour notes to a more researched, documented text in which I have tried to balance two goals. First, while I didn't want to create a text book, I did want to present a basic record of what was there when we arrived, what we found when we were doing the work, and what we left when we were finished. This has been like a treasure hunt because I love both the history and the stories, and I have learned so much that I want to share. Each time I sat down to write, it seemed some new piece of information had sent me looking for more information that I added to text that I thought I had already finished.

An example of this is my decision to refer to the building as The Governor's House instead of The Governor's Mansion or The Executive Mansion. I used "The Executive Mansion" just because everyone called it that. As I continued writing, I began to think about how agricultural properties of the period had descriptive names like Mount Vernon or Monticello and houses in the city were merely referred to as someone's house, such as the Lee House. Even John Wickham's home, far more elaborate with its circular stair entry, friezes, and decorative wall murals, is generally just called the Wickham House. I also found that the description "Governor's House" is confirmed in vouchers, inventories, and building reports from the 19th century. Monies that were appropriated from the Legislature were described as being for the Government or Governor's House. Inventories, like "A List of Furniture etc. in the Governor's House on 17th April 1823," are clear in calling it the Governor's House. Not only is the reference to a house, but the list of meager furnishings show that it was hardly a mansion as we imagine one. Moreover, the Legislature had rejected Thomas Jefferson's design of a "governor's palace," and only years later under pressure appropriated funds for the construction of an adequate "dwelling for a family" that Governor John Tyler seemed to expect. It was not until later in the 19th century and into the early 20th that Governor's Mansion or Executive Mansion began to be commonly used.

It is this "dwelling for a family" aspect that I believe has always held true. Above all it is a home for a family, albeit one that represents all families in Virginia. Our sons, Jay and Ashton, spent important growing years here, doing all the things other children do–inviting friends over, learning to drive, playing guitars. They had the added benefit of getting to know the people who, though they were assigned to work at the house, were in the end really more like family. Tutti, Juan, Maria, and Marian all made day to day life a pleasure. Jay and Ashton spent hours with the troopers in the EPU office and were fascinated by how the security squad worked, but more impressed by their kindness. Others whose jobs were really related to tours and official duties, Stacy Hight, Amy Finch, and Jessica Clark, went beyond their scheduling and management duties and were companions as well. And Chef Mark Herndon and *sous* chefs Thomas Sauers and Sarah Everidge made certain that meals were excellent and served in the time frame of a family juggling official duties and normal daily life.

But in the end I didn't think of the Governor's House as a place for just our family; it is truly a house for all Virginia families. I saw that in the many times the house was open to the public and parents joined us on holidays, bringing their children to see the Christmas tree or sitting with children dressed in Halloween costume who listened wide-eyed to our ghost story in the front yard and squealed as an apparition appeared in an upstairs window. I particularly saw the interest that people paid in the work we did during the restoration. Downtown workers on lunch break would come and stand at the fence, watching the construction as if it were at their own homes. They worried about whether we were removing historic glass and other features that they believed should be maintained. They provided information about history that they knew and believed was important to the house. And most telling, many stood for hours when we had the grand opening on New Year's Day, 2000, to see their house and what we had done. It was all of these observations that brought me back to the conclusion that this is a house, and a home, and that calling it the Governor's House completely conveys that image.

The second important purpose of this book is to support those who undertake historic preservation and thus parts of Virginia's history. This includes not only major sites like Colonial Williamsburg, Historic Jamestowne and Mount Vernon, to mention a very few of a vast number, but also individuals who strive to save a small piece of the past in a home or storefront. When a few of us made an earlier attempt to record our house restoration efforts, some people eagerly pointed out that our enthusiasm, and perhaps our use of a hyperbole or two to tell the story, was over-zealous. We were told that while "the Mansion is indeed a National Historic Landmark, . . . most would agree that the state Capitol is a more significant structure, both architecturally and historically. Indeed, two other Virginia places: Monticello and Jefferson's Academical Village are on the World Heritage List. We all like the Mansion, but we need to be honest about it." In other words, they said, get real, the importance of the Mansion just doesn't measure up to other historic sites, especially the Jeffersonian ones.

I couldn't disagree with this sentiment more. Granted, as an architect Alexander Parris was no Thomas Jefferson. Nor is the Mansion on the scale of Monticello, and its purpose not on the level of the Capitol or The University. But putting forward the idea that a piece of history is less important because it is not the major piece misses the reality of how it is the small pieces of history that tell the whole story. As an ancient historian I understand the frustration of knowing the part of the story that survived in the record, yet long for the nuances that the overlooked or lost ordinary stories would tell us today. It is as if to say a symphony would be as fulfilling if the orchestra played only the tune. And so I have persevered to complete this book in the hope that what I record will in some way help fill in at least part of the story.

Virginia has an abundance of historic homes and buildings that boast exquisite craftsmanship and materials besides those at our major historical sites. Many of these buildings are being lost to decay or have features that are being lost to faster, more economical means of salvage. But the talent it took to design these structures and to produce such beautiful woodwork, not to mention the rich woods themselves, deserve to be preserved and passed on for others to enjoy. These houses should serve as a link to the past and all that Virginians contributed to our nation's development. I urge anyone who wishes to save a historic structure to follow the Secretary of the Interior's Standards for the Treatment of Historic Properties in order to stay within accepted guidelines for preservation.

However, historic preservation is not for the easily discouraged. Problems are frequent, often unexpected, and just as often expensive. But the rewards are fulfilling, giving not just a tangible result, but a genuine sense of accomplishment in saving something worthwhile. Though this work is not a manual or a step by step guide to preservation, I have tried to present some of the major issues we encountered on our project that are frequently grappled with in conservation efforts, and to explain what processes we used to decide how we would address these problems. We followed the standards of preservation and used contractors that also adhered to those standards. We remained committed to recording information that we found about earlier periods at the house. We were assisted in those efforts by the Virginia Department of Historic Resources which participated actively in the project. They worked to create a daily record of activities at the site, hiring Sadler and Whitehead, Architects, PLC, to photograph each day's work and what we found throughout the entire project. Still photographs and video images were taken by Mary Harding Sadler and Joseph D. Lahendro and are available for online viewing on the website of the Library of Virginia. Their record has been invaluable to me as I have tried to reconstruct and discuss our efforts, and it will help anyone that works on the house in the future. We sometimes found it difficult to proceed because we didn't know exactly what we were going to find in an area. The Governor's House is a "living" building, and as long as families live there and there are daily activities there, there will be an ongoing need to maintain and upgrade the facilities. Having their record and my meager narrative will hopefully make the process of maintenance easier and prevent the building from deteriorating as dramatically as it had before we arrived.

But the most important aspect of all of this that I want to convey is that this was a team project. To be sure, there were so many who helped bring this job in on time and under budget that it is impossible to name them all. But I know the excitement we all had when we found the handwritten notes from workers who had performed some task earlier in the life of the house, and I wanted in some way to acknowledge that it was the efforts of our team that led to the success of the restoration. Though all of the individual's names may not appear here, the work of all was nonetheless of critical value and greatly appreciated. I say thank you to everyone.

As for writing this book, I have received help from many friends and people who have become friends during this process. Some have been on this whole journey, from restoration through book. Many who were deeply involved in the restoration in the Department of General Services have tried to guide me to finding correct data and to make sure I have stated things correctly; Trev Crider, Bruce Brooks, Tony Griffin, John Mitchell and Donald C. Williams were all generous with their time and resources. At the Department of Historic Resources (DHR), now led by Kathryn Kilpatrick, I have found unhesitating assistance. Diane "Dee" Deroche always welcomed me to work with the artifacts and documents there, and Caitlyn O'Grady provided images of the archaeological finds. Cara Metz, the archaeologist who excavated and documented the historic elements we uncovered, discussed the finds and reviewed my observations along the way. Also willing to listen to my questions and offer support was Bill Crosby who had been DHR's representative at all of the meetings while the project was underway.

John D. Metz, Director of Collections Management Services, and Minor Weisiger, Archives Research Coordinator, at the Library of Virginia helped me explore the vouchers, inventories and other primary sources about the Governor's House and Capitol Square that are maintained in the archives there. John was extremely generous with his time as I endlessly wanted to discuss questions I had about architectural changes throughout the life of the house. Dale Neighbors, Coordinator of the Prints and Photographs collection at the library, and Paige Buchbinder kindly helped me find the illustrations available for the

Governor's House. Blending text and photos gave me the wonderful opportunity to become reacquainted with Mark Fagerburg, who had taken photos during the project for the Library of Virginia. Donna Case, House Director while we were there and an active participant in the restoration, helped me remember the arrangement of the house and the day to day activities there. She was also nice enough to read portions of the text and check for the accuracy of my recollections. Tracy Kamerer, now the Chief Curator at the Flagler Museum in Palm Beach, was tremendously supportive in reading and making suggestions.

Barbara Strickland Page was not just the interior design expert for the restoration, but she became a friend after the many trips we took–to the Scalamandre mill in New York, to the Design Studio in Washington– to explore all the possibilities of furnishings for the house. We share a love of classical design and beautiful fabrics. Barbara and I both admire the tremendous talents of Ruth Hubbard and Kathryn Arnold of the Colonial Williamsburg Design Studio, and the four of us have enjoyed getting together to talk about the fun time we all had while the project was underway. I appreciate the help they all have given me in getting this current task completed.

But I also had a great deal of help with individuals not in state service or directly involved in the renovation. William J. Martin, Director of the Valentine Richmond History Center which maintains the Wickham House, gave me unending access to their huge collection of photographs, news articles and books, a large number of which focus on the Governor's House and the families that have lived there. Meg Hughes and August Reinhardt Simpson guided me through their files and were always kind, answering my never ending questions and listening to my frequent exclamation, "Look at that!"

My sister, Mary Jane Black, and of course Jim, Jay and Ashton, all said "press on" when it looked like the project had stalled. It would never have been finished without their encouragement.

I have learned through this process that writers cannot be proud. Charlie Finley with Verbatim Editing and Pat Smith at Dietz Press know far too much now about my shortcomings with the comma, and I appreciated their polite suggestions about grammar and content.

Despite everything that I have learned, the one thing I clearly understand now is that there is still more to be learned and recorded about the house. There is still more to be written about changes that have already occurred, and there will be more to write as new first families come and go. I have tried to be correct and present some of the new evidence that we found that may shed light on events of the past. I hope that what I have included in this volume will give some future writer a sound base of information and a place to begin.

Roxane Gatling Gilmore

For Jim, Jay and Ashton
Forsan et haec olim meminisse juvabit.   Vergil, *The Aeneid I.203.*

CHAPTER 1

Alexander Parris Designs a Governor's House

When Virginia developed its governmental systems as a new commonwealth at the end of the American Revolution, its seat of governing remained in Williamsburg. Those serving in Virginia government continued to use the same Capitol and Governor's Palace in Williamsburg that had been used by the British royal governors. When Virginia's capital moved from Williamsburg to Richmond in 1780, Thomas Jefferson put much effort into designing the area now known as Capitol Square. Jefferson planned an elaborate complex of buildings for Richmond that included not only a new Capitol but a Governor's "palace" as well.

Jefferson was inspired in his design of the Capitol by the Maison Carrée in Nîmes, France, which he considered one of the most perfect buildings that he visited while he lived in Europe in 1785. Jefferson reflected on his love for this Augustan Roman temple in a letter that he wrote to Madame La Comtesse de Tessé, the older cousin of Lafayette, whom Jefferson frequently visited while in Paris.

> Here I am, Madam, gazing whole hours at the Maison Quarrée, like a lover at his mistress. The stocking weavers and silk spinners around it consider me a hypochondriac Englishman, about to write with a pistol the last chapter of his history. This is the second time I have been in love since I left Paris.[1]

Jefferson employed Charles Louis Clérisseau to develop a plan for the Capitol based on his beloved temple. Clérisseau had an artist, Jean-Pierre Fouquet, construct a stucco model for the temple, showing the changes in the columns and the addition of features such as windows to accommodate modern usage.[2]

The Maison Carrée in Nîmes, France inspired Jefferson in his design of the Capitol. Adaptations for usage such as windows were shown on a model that he ordered built.

Jefferson not only loved the lines of Greek and Roman structures, but he believed that the use of classical architecture gave instant gravity to the elements he was trying to build–a fledgling nation, a state, and The University of Virginia.

In September 1785 Jefferson wrote from Paris that he was an enthusiast of the arts. "But it is an enthusiasm of which I am not ashamed, as its object is to improve the taste of my countrymen, to increase their reputation, to reconcile to them the respect of the world, and procure them its praise. . . ."[3] This declaration in support of the arts was Jefferson's reaction to the news that the building of the Capitol in Richmond had begun without consideration of his plan to use the Maison Carrée as its model. Jefferson was despondent after learning that ground had been broken on the Capitol without his plan having been considered. In a letter from Paris, Jefferson implored his friend, James Madison, to intercede for the construction of this copy of "the most beautiful and precious morsel of architecture left us by antiquity."

"It is very simple, but it is noble beyond expression, and would have done honor to our country, as presenting to travelers a specimen in taste in our infancy, promising much for our maturer age."[4] Eventually Jefferson's wishes were granted, and the Capitol in the image of his precious Maison Carrée, was completed sufficiently for use by 1788.

Jefferson's designs for Capitol Square were not limited to the Capitol building itself. Earlier, when the Capital moved to Richmond, Jefferson's residence as governor from April 1780 to June 1781 was in quarters outside Capitol Square rented from his uncle Thomas Turpin, Sr., who had married Jefferson's aunt, Mary Jefferson.[5] This house may have stood on the corner of Broad and Governor Streets on the site where the Memorial Hospital was later constructed. When he began work on his plans for Capitol Square, Jefferson included an equally elaborate "Governor's Palace" to stand alongside his perfect Capitol. Perhaps his idea was to represent the separation of powers with an architectural statement. Perhaps it was to give the governor status on a par with the legislature. Whatever his reasons for wanting such a magnificent design, and whatever the real reasons of the legislature for rejecting them, in the end economic conditions prevented its construction, and governors continued to live in various temporary quarters. (Jefferson's drawings are available in the Coolidge Collection at the Massachusetts Historical Society.)

Few records are left concerning the Richmond residences of governors from 1780 to 1813. At some unknown date a small frame structure, already built on the property purchased for the Capitol, was expected to be used by governors for their residence. However old the building at its acquisition, it soon was reported to be run-down and unsuitable for living. Building and furnishings alike were said to be "ruined," with chairs described as "old and many of them broken."[6] Billing records indicate the frame structure was constantly being whitewashed and rooms altered and added to in order to accommodate living. Many governors did not live there at all, preferring to stay in their own local residences.

Samuel Mordecai writes in his *Reminiscences of an Old Citizen* in 1860 the following words about the first Richmond Governor's House.

The Governor's House preceding the present one, was a very plain wooden building of two stories, with only two moderate sized rooms on the first floor. It was for many years unconscious of paint and the furniture was in keeping with the republican simplicity of the edifice, and of its occupants, from Henry and Jefferson down to Monroe and Page. The railings around the yard were usually in a dilapidated condition, and the goats that sported on the steep hill-sides of the Capitol Square, claimed and exercised the liberty of grazing on his Excellency's grounds.[7]

Though there are no detailed records of this first structure beyond this description of Mordecai, there may be one depiction of the house in the background of a 1797 Benjamin Latrobe watercolor of Capitol Square. Latrobe's image shows a building with at least two chimneys and a porch that appears to open out onto Governor Street.[8] The building is labeled *The Governor's House* in the painting.

We hoped that some evidence of this early building would be found during the 1999 renovation, but none was evident. There was excitement over a pocket of artifacts that workmen found when excavation was done in 1999 for a new gate into the current Governor's House grounds at about the location of the house in the Latrobe watercolor. A brick foundation was found beneath the existing wall, and the Department of Historic Resources, led by Cara Metz, archaeologist, examined the finds. It is now believed that what was found may have been the foundation of a smokehouse that appears on an early plan of the Capitol grounds. Within this foundation there was a pocket of artifacts, deposited at some unknown time, either as fill for the foundation, or as a trash pit at some time when the building was no longer being used. Even the occupants of the Governor's House had to deal with disposing of their trash, and this spot may have served that purpose.

Some of the artifacts found in this salvage excavation were early–such as a white salt-glazed stoneware teapot lid with overglazed accents that may have been used by the royal governors in the Palace in Wil-

This Parian teapot lid was found in a large deposit of artifacts [EM 44HE9511] discovered in January 1999 while excavating a new West Gate entry into the grounds. Cara Metz, right, directed the salvage archaeology for DHR.

Courtesy DHR

Alexander Parris Designs a Governor's House

liamsburg. Jefferson had been criticized for continuing to use furnishings that had been brought from the Palace, giving some weight to the Williamsburg origin of some early ceramic pieces. But other numerous fragments of china including multitudes of Blue Willow patterns indicate that the contents of the fill were from many administrations. A Tam O'Shanter pitcher dated October 1, 1835 tells us that the deposit cannot date earlier than that date.[9]

Wherever it stood, the final complaint about the condition of this first Richmond "mansion" seems to have come from John Tyler, governor from December 1808 to January 1811. In his report to the Legislature in December 1810, he states that:

> the governor's tenement is going fast to destruction, having been originally badly built and is too small for a family. The patch-work which has adorned it for 20 years has cost greatly more than a good durable brick building would have done.... The present situation is intolerable for a private family, there being not a foot of ground that is not exposed to three streets, besides a cluster of dirty tenements immediately in front of this house, with their windows opening into the enclosure.[10]

His observations must have been uncontested since it is remarkable that money would be appropriated for a governor's residence with a British invasion imminent on the eve of the War of 1812.

In 1811 the General Assembly appropriated $50 to hire Alexander Parris, a Boston architect, to draw plans for a new house for the state's chief executive.[11] Parris had come to Richmond to build his practice and was designing other homes in the area, most notably the nearby residence of wealthy businessman, John Wickham. The Assembly did not envision a residence on the scale of Jefferson's original plan, or one as elaborate as the Wickham House. Their idea was to provide for the "comfort and convenience of the Governor" and at the same time reflect the "honor and dignity of the State."[12] On February 13, 1811, an Act of the General Assembly appropriated $12,000 for the construction of Parris' design. A Memorandum of Agreement dated March, 1, 1811, between William Moncure and A.B. Venable to rent Moncure's house and grounds for the use of the Governor, was witnessed by Alexander Parris.[13] Parris delivered his plans for a new house which Christopher Tompkins, a Richmond builder, was hired to construct.

By 1813, at a cost of $18,871.82, the Governor's House was completed. The initial appropriation by the Legislature, $12,000, was increased in February 1812 by $8,000 to include changes in the Parris plan. Two side porches and a structure replacing dilapidated outbuildings with one two-story brick servants' quarters and Kitchen, not part of Parris' design, were added in this first construction period. This outbuilding now referred to as "the Cottage," still stands and is used as a guest house.

At the end of the building phase, the Governor's House was prepared for occupancy and the final costs for labor and construction were determined through a formal measurement process that was used at the time. Independent "referees" for the owner, the Commonwealth, and the builder, Christopher Tompkins, were used to evaluate the costs based on set formulas for each craftsman on the project. Billing receipts show that Alexander McKim, the commonwealth's agent, was paid $60 for this service, and that Wilson Bryan was the representative for Tompkins. The house itself, materials included, was valued at $14,525.53, and the Kitchen, smokehouse, necessary, fencing and land improvements were valued at $3,986.29. Since the total appropriation had been $20,000, the remaining sum, $1,128.18, was designated to be used partially for finishing an enclosure.[14]

The Cottage, not part of Parris' original plans, was built the house to replace other dilapidated buildings. It served as a kitchen and servants quarters.
Courtesy DHR

Concluding the Report of the Commissioners was their opinion that "the exterior view of the building, the comfort and the conveniency (sic) of its habitants, would be greatly encreased (sic) by the superstructure of a terrace surrounding the eaves of the building, and of a portico to the door fronting the Capitol; that to the fire places, marble hearths and slabs ought to be substituted for the plain (now standing) brick ones . . . ."[15] They also opined that additional property should be purchased to give sufficient ground for a garden, stable and carriage house to replace the existing dilapidated one. Though this statement supports the idea that the structure was built as a house and not a palace as Jefferson had envisioned it, it also shows that even before its first resident had arrived, there were already additional projects being recommended for the house and grounds, an endeavor that goes on to this day.

After months of watching with interest the progress of the Governor's House construction, Governor James Barbour and his family moved into the new structure in March 1813. Ever since Barbour became its first occupant, all Virginia governors and their families have lived in this third House, making it the oldest U.S. governor's house still in use *as a residence*. Kentucky has a house older than the Virginia Governor's House where their governors used to live, but it no longer serves that purpose. The first Virginia Governor's residence, the colonial Governor's Palace, was reconstructed in Williamsburg in the 1930s and can be visited on tours. The reconstruction of The Governor's Palace and other buildings in Williamsburg by the Rockefeller Foundation set the standard for historic preservation in America, and our 1998 restoration of the Richmond Governor's House adhered to these standards.

The second, dilapidated residence was torn down while the Parris-designed Governor's House was under construction. There is an April 20, 1811 record of sale to Chs. Copland at the request of an Act of the Assembly for "the house which the former governor resided." A December 24, 1956 handwritten note by Mrs. Francis Waring Robinson of Lakeville, Connecticut records that her "ancestor Charles Copland, resident at the S.W. corner of Broad and 11th (if my memory is correct on this location) purchased the materials of the 'Old Governor's Palace' April 20, 1811 for $530, when it was torn down and replaced." Her note is on file at the Richmond History Center. Copland apparently did not remove the entire structure, and newspaper advertisements recorded the offer for sale of the remainder of the materials.

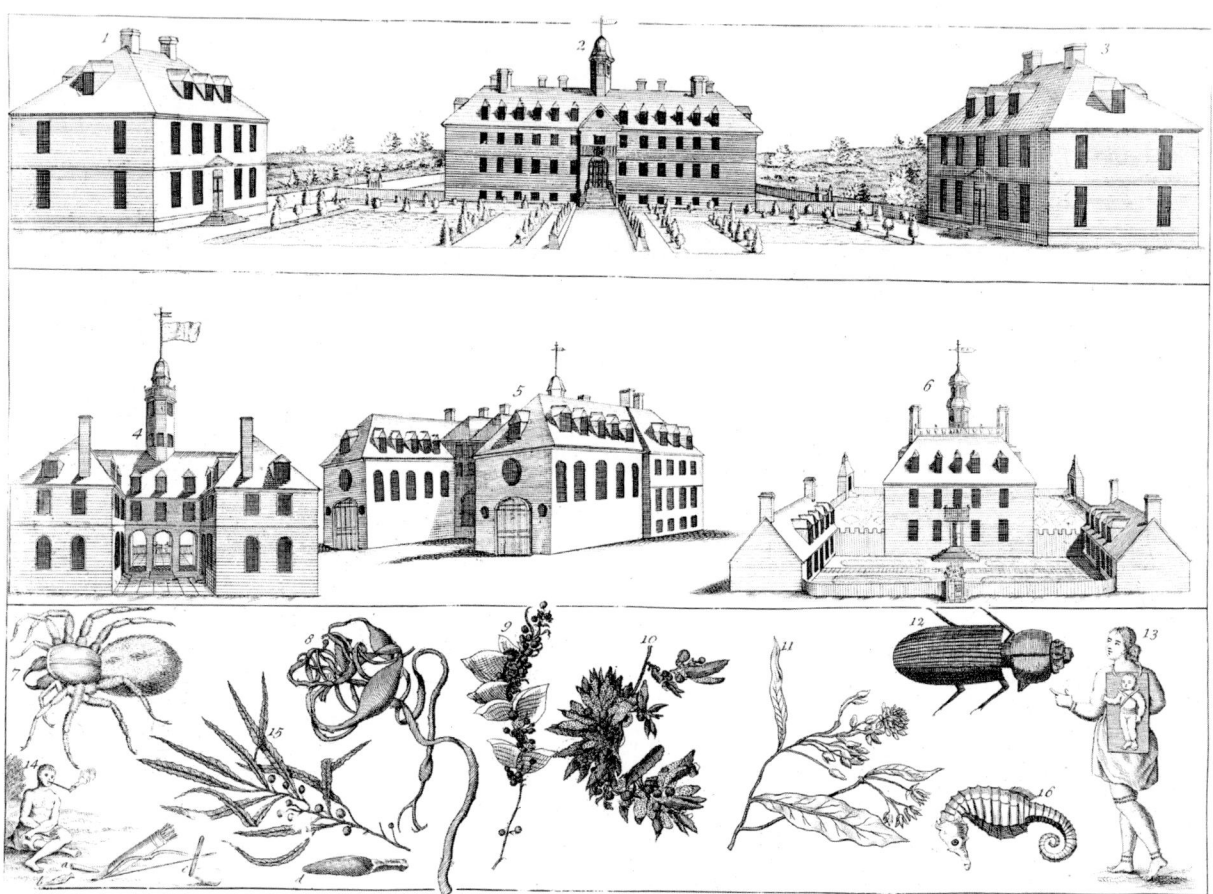

This 1740s copperplate, known as the Bodleian Plate, shows the Williamsburg Governor's Palace (middle row, right image) before it was destroyed by fire in 1781. Governors from Henry through Jefferson resided here before the capital moved to Richmond.

Courtesy The Colonial Williamsburg Foundation

Parris' Boston origins are seen in his 1826 pencil sketch of the Governor's House, the earliest known depiction of the completed house.[16] The influence of the work of Bostonian architect Charles Bulfinch is pronounced in this sketch by Parris. Frontal symmetry with an arched central doorway and double window over the doorway, and panels between window courses are reminiscent of Bulfinch's Harrison Otis Gray House. Though the Parris sketch shows the panels plain, from the early 1820s through the Civil War, these panels were embellished with plaster decorations of floral and ribbon swags.

The interior of the Parris Governor's House was a fairly typical Federal style house dominated by the symmetry of its rooms and features. His hand-drawn floor plan shows two basically identical front parlors separated by a large Entry Hall. The entry ended with an archway where there were hallways to north and south staircases. Also at the end of the entry were two doors leading to two identical rooms on the east side of the house. Parris labeled the southeast room as the Dining Room and the northeast room as the Drawing Room. In the sketch these two rooms are joined in the center of the building by a broad doorway.

The Parris sketch was most likely his early proposal of how the house should be built, with the final plans changing as the building got underway. Close examination of the sketch shows that the house as built differs in one way that we know must have been changed as the building was constructed. The fireplaces, located on the exterior of the building in the sketch are on the interior of the finished building. Parris seemed to like to place fireplaces on the exterior of buildings, a feature that Benjamin Latrobe criti-

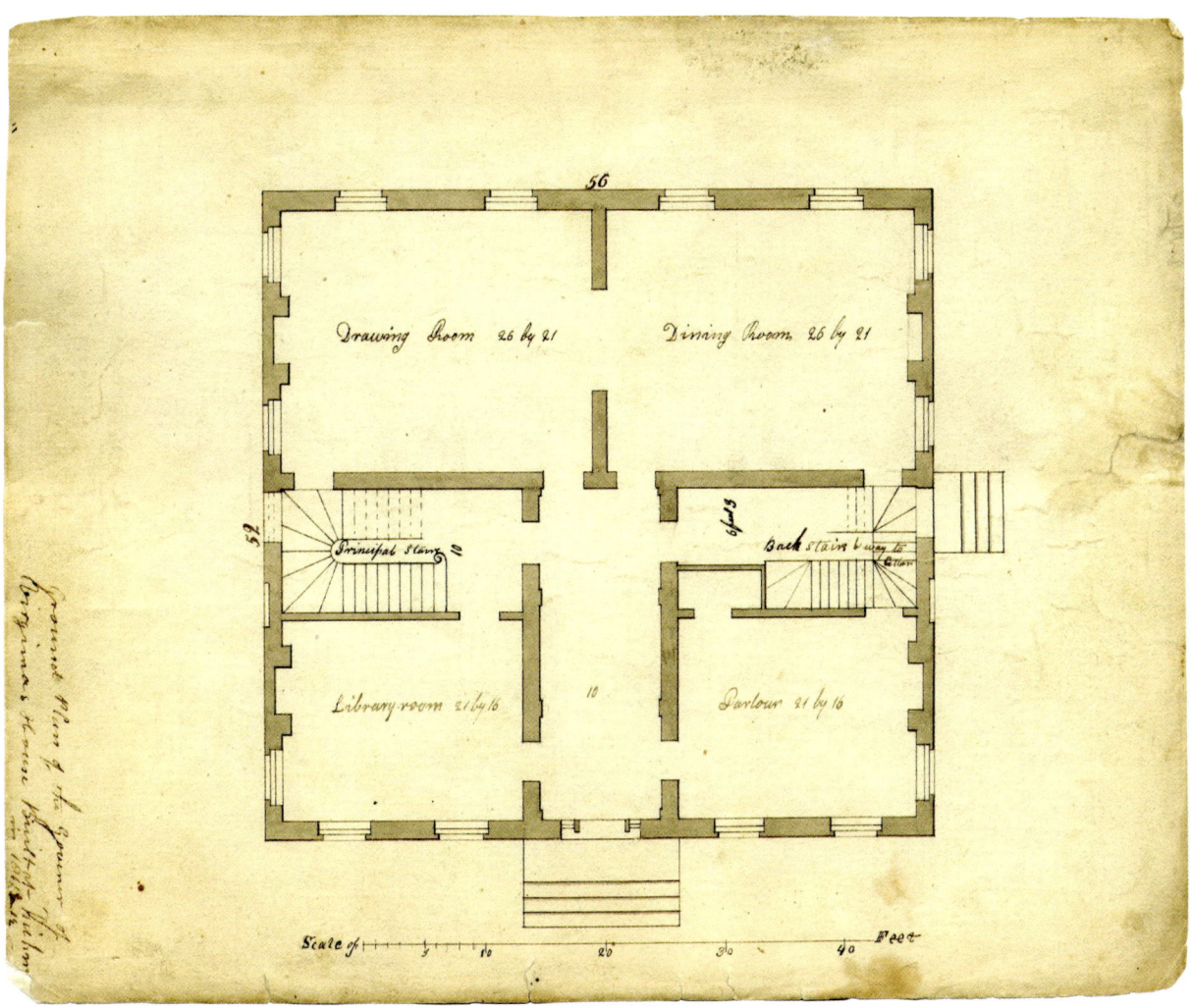

While basically built as shown, Alexander Parris' only known drawing of the Governor's House shows its fireplaces along the exterior northern and southern walls, not where they were finally located in the center of the structure. This change must have been made during the original construction. With the exception of that change, this basic plan remained until the dramatic alterations of Duncan Lee in 1906.

Courtesy of the American Antiquarian Society

Alexander Parris Designs a Governor's House

cized him for when Latrobe assessed his design of the Wickham House. We can only speculate whether it was this criticism that led Parris to change the location of the fireplaces in the Governor's House, but whatever his reason, the house was built with its fireplaces on the interior. While the change in the location of the fireplaces is a readily apparent change, other changes are more complicated to analyze and beg further study.

The staircases to both the second floor and basement have undergone numerous changes over the life of the house. Their current locations, put into their final form by Governor Henry Carter Stuart in 1914, are on the opposite walls (east) from where they are in the sketch (west). This change in location would have affected the hallway parlor doors as well as the vestibules leading to the side porticos. During our repair of the side hallway floors and walls, we found "ghosts" of the Parris staircases along the west walls where they are shown in his sketch and the remains of floor openings for the basement stair. A focused study of these alterations might give a picture of how and why they were made and how they affected the vestibules at the side entrances. When the patches to the floor openings were made, they were done with wainscot

The Entry Hall as designed by Parris is shown decorated for a 1905 visit by President Theodore Roosevelt. Of particular note is the partition behind the arch separating the rear parlors from the front of the house. The wreathed torch in the corner of the ceiling is also visible.

Courtesy The Cook Collection, Valentine Richmond History Center no longer needed for the walls. Quality materials were seldom just discarded, but were recycled to best advantage. We continued that practice using pieces of the discovered wainscot to repair places in the Old Governor's Office.

A series of photographs taken to record the visit of President Theodore Roosevelt to Richmond in 1905 is the only known pictorial documentation of all of the first floor rooms of the Governor's House in the basic Parris design as it existed before the sweeping interior changes of Duncan Lee in 1906.

One photograph shows the Parris grand Entry Hall that was flanked by identical front parlors. Though the house lacked the frills that adorned the Wickham House, plaster friezes and a stately, beaded arch decorated the hall. The ornamental frieze surrounding the ceiling was a popular pattern of the period that boasted torches, draped urns and connecting foliage. It still embellishes the hall today. The photograph also shows that the ceiling had a plaster border around its perimeter and in each corner was a torch within what appears to be a laurel wreath. The hall ended with a beaded, arched wall that had two doors, each entering into separate Drawing Rooms on the back of the house. These doors, decorated with bunting, are shown in the photo.

Two other photographs show the front parlors, identical and mirroring each other across the hallway. Fireplaces were located along the interior walls of the rooms. The room ceilings were adorned with plasterwork that still remains, more delicate in its features than the bold plaster seen in the hallway. In the corners of these borders are crossed torches and ribbons.

On the rear of the first floor were the Parris Drawing Room and Dining Room, entered through the two arched doorways from the grand hall. A previously unpublished photograph of the first floor shows these two rooms joined in the center of the house by a broad doorway. Like the front parlors these rear Drawing Rooms had interior fireplaces. The ceiling perimeters were decorated with the same delicate plaster borders of crossed torches and ribbons seen in the front parlors. Unlike the ceiling decorations of the front parlors, those in the rear did not survive Duncan Lee's changes to the first floor.

Tales and memories of the residents of the Governor's House provide some idea of how the Parris de-

LEFT: *The Governor's Office in 1905 still had a marble fireplace. It was flanked by doors leading to a side hallway between the office and a rear parlor.* RIGHT: *The Ladies' Parlor was a mirror image of the Governor's Office. The newly installed parquet floor is visible.*

Courtesy The Cook Collection, Valentine Richmond History Center

Alexander Parris Designs a Governor's House

This previously unpublished photograph shows the two Parris rear parlors as they existed before being changed into the Ballroom by Duncan Lee. While the center doorway is shown taken at the time of Roosevelt's visit, in the Parris sketch of the rooms, some believe it was added later by Governor "Extra Billy" Smith. Ceiling decorations are also visible here but did not survive the Lee changes.

Courtesy The Cook Collection, Valentine Richmond History Center

signed residence was used through its first century, though often these stories create as many questions as they answer, both about the design of the house and the events that happened there. One of the biggest questions raised is whether the doorway between the rear parlors was actually constructed by Alexander Parris or added by Governor "Extra Billy" Smith in 1846. Much supports the doorway's original existence.

The original Parris drawing for the House shows the two back parlors joined by a broad doorway, and this is the very configuration that is observed in the 1905 photograph. Inventories confirm that the northern back parlor was referred to frequently as the Drawing Room, the very name Parris uses on the sketch. There are tales of governors retreating to this back space for meetings. The southern back parlor was originally used as the dining room, and was designated as such on the sketch. Bowls of "punch" were left by Governors on the sideboard of the Dining Room to greet dry throated visitors while business was conducted in the governor's office or adjacent Drawing Room.

But stories and records of the changes at the house by Governor Smith from March 1, 1846 to December 31, 1848 in the use of the back parlors raise questions about the original first floor design of Alexander Parris and whether the central doorway was omitted or was smaller than shown. During this time Smith is

10   Restoring the Virginia Governor's House

reported to have moved the Dining Room to the basement, and at the same time a "broad door was cut" and "sliding doors added" between what had been the Dining Room and the back parlor, thus "foreshadowing the current Ballroom."[17]

The report of Smith moving the Dining Room to the basement seems correct since that was the dining room's location when Duncan Lee moved it back to the main floor in 1906. A December 31, 1848 inventory refers to both an "Upper Dining Room" and a "Lower Dining Room," showing that at least a transition to basement dining was underway. This inventory shows there were 42 chairs in the upper Dining Room though it does not list a table. In the lower Dining Room there were 4 tables and 16 chairs, seeming to indicate that the upper room was perhaps for receptions and the lower room for meals. First Lady Etta Donnan Mann mentions in her memoirs in 1910 that the dining room had at one time been in the basement. While all of these records confirm Governor Smith moved dining to the basement, whether he cut the door between the two upper rooms is not as clear. The payment vouchers and an 1846 report about Capitol Square buildings to Governor Smith by the Superintendent of Public Edifices, Charles Dimmock, do not answer the question, and the 1905 photograph only seems to increase the mystery.

An October 3, 1846 payment voucher to Wm. Forbes, shows that an existing door was removed and framing for a new door with jambs and fluted pilasters was added. The same voucher also provided for "large sliding doors," and "floor and framing in place of partition wall." However, the voucher does not say on what floor the door was removed or where the sliding doors were added. The rest of the voucher deals with work that was being done in the basement and to the south portico and passageway to the Kitchen. Thus, the two doors could be other work done in the basement, though vouchers frequently contained itemized entries for work done in multiple areas.

Like the voucher, Superintendent Dimmock's report specifies only work that was done in the basement. His report states as a general observation that the house was "overhauled, put in good order, the interior modernized, painted, papered, partially new carpet, furnaces for warming the lower rooms, new portico to the south end of the main building, a covered way from the house to the Kitchen...." He goes on to say that "two basement rooms were finished for family occupation." While there is no specific description of the new doors, and Dimmock says that the work was done at the request of the Governor and so didn't need more detail in his report, most of the substantive changes seem to have been in the basement.

Finally, while the 1905 photograph confirms that there was a broad doorway between the two rooms, it does not shed any light on when it was installed. The picture shows a broad door with fluted pilasters and a large cap over the doorway. The floor here would have had to have been repaired if a partition had been removed there. (The parquet floor shown in the picture was added in 1903. Since it postdates both Parris and Lee, it is not part of the question in this discussion. The original flooring beneath the parquet is what might shed light on how this area was changed.) The 1846 voucher mentions fluted pilasters, large caps, and flooring repairs. But all of those are features that would have been used because they matched Parris' design throughout the first floor; they would have been there if Parris had installed the door.

However, the items mentioned in the voucher that are not apparent in the photograph are the "large sliding doors." In the voucher these doors seem linked to the pilasters, jambs and floor repair materials, so one would expect to find them in this doorway if it is the one Smith had altered. Unless another governor removed Smith's sliding doors, they should still be there at the time of this photograph, unless all Smith

This death mask of General Thomas ""Stonewall" Jackson was made in 1863 by Frederick Volck when Jackson's body was brought to the Governor's House and prepared to lie in state at the Capitol.
Courtesy Valentine Richmond History Center

did was to install an open doorway there. We must wonder where, if not in this doorway, were these sliding doors installed? Is it possible that the rooms were always joined by a broad door as is in fact shown in the original Parris sketch. Perhaps when Smith moved the dining room to the basement it was necessary to add doors to the two basement rooms that Superintendent Dimmock said were "finished for family occupation." While no apparent physical evidence for the separation of these two basement rooms was found during the renovation (see Chapter 11), there is no doubt that basement space had to be altered in order to accommodate formal dining for the first time. The voucher and superintendent's statement indicate as much, and the fact that there were two rooms being changed in the basement corresponds with the two doors discussed in the voucher. Smith's changes on the first floor may have been the papering with the lavish Killarney Frescoe wallpaper that is mentioned in other vouchers from fall of 1846.

Whenever they were joined by the double doorway, two well-known events to happen at the Governor's House show the back parlors being used as an open, end-to-end space by 1863, the date of one of the most dramatic events to occur at the Governor's House. In May 1863, the body of Stonewall Jackson lay in state in the "large reception room."[18] It is reported that once the body was in the house, it was finally "properly embalmed" and a death mask made, after which lines of official visitors paid their respects to the fallen general. The parade was stopped by Governor Letcher only by the lateness of the hour. The next day, the coffin was carried from the Governor's House, down Governor Street to Main, back up the hill to Ninth Street and into the Grace Street entrance of Capitol Square in a trip that took one and a half hours. While the body of the general lay in state at the Capitol, Mrs. Jackson was reported to be resting at the Governor's Mansion in a darkened parlor.[19] The "large reception room" no doubt refers to the connected, rear parlors. No positive identification can be made about where Mrs. Jackson was resting, though it could have been one of the small parlors on the front of the house.

The only known picture of either of the original back parlors while in use is a photograph of a children's party during the administration of Governor Andrew Jackson Montague. It is said that on February 22, 1903, a party was held to celebrate the birthday of George Washington, one of Virginia's most famous sons.[20] Ten-year-old Gay Montague, daughter of the Governor, and her guests were dressed as young George and Martha Washingtons, complete with powdered wigs and hooped skirts. The picture shows the southeast back parlor and about 80 young guests posed for the camera.

While the picture shows that a spirited event did indeed occur at the house, it is left to our imagination how a party of this sort unfolded, and some of the story does raise questions. It was reported that the "parents filled the little parlor and sitting room as spectators, while the double parlors . . . presented a polished

12 Restoring the Virginia Governor's House

oak floor for the minuets, reels, and figures."[21] The double parlors would have indeed acted as a single, large space for what must have been a lively event. By the time of the Montague administration the dining room was in the basement of the house, so there would have been no issue of dining room furniture impeding the dancing.

But the rest of the story raises some interesting questions. The little parlor and sitting room must refer to the smaller, front rooms; but, even in the modern, open Governor's House it is impossible to be a spectator of events in the back of the house from the front parlors. In the original Parris design, still in place at this time, the partition from the arched doorways in the hall to the back would have obstructed views into the back even more.

It was also reported that guards were posted to protect freezers of ice cream stored there in "deep snow" for "several days before the party." They were distracted from their duty because they were looking through the windows at the dancers in the back parlors and all but one freezer of ice cream was stolen by town boys.[22] However, there are no windows that reach close enough to the ground for anyone to peer through them and view an activity in any room on the first floor, especially the back Drawing Rooms, thus making

Gay Montague and friends celebrate the birthday of George Washington in February 1903.

the ice cream guards' alibi remarkable. Even more remarkable is that National Weather Service records show that while there was 9.8 inches of snow in February 1902, there was only two-tenths of an inch for the entire month of February 1903 making the reports of stored ice cream curious indeed.[23]

No matter how colorful the repeated tale, it is these embellished stories of life at the Governor's House, combined with its architectural history that made the restoration of the House important to me as First Lady. Though Lafayette may never have slept in the "Lafayette Bedroom," his visit to the Governor's House and the visits of so many other dignitaries, family friends, senators and delegates plus the countless hours that staff members have spent keeping the house in order throughout its two hundred year existence made this a living building, worthy of preservation.

Though its proportions are not correct, this lithograph by E. Sachs & Co of the "Governors House of Richmond VA." was a widely circulated image of the Governor's House in the mid-19th century. A notation in the lower left corner of the print says that it was "Drawn from nature by Frederick Diehlman." The drawing shows the balustrade, parapet and side panels that were added in the 1830s to Parris' originally unadorned exterior. These features were removed after the Civil War because of the expense of maintaining them. They were returned by the Baliles administration in the 1980s.

Courtesy Library of Virginia

14 Restoring the Virginia Governor's House

CHAPTER 2

The Governor's House Changes with Time

*I*n the early days of Virginia, many houses were constructed based on the idea that a single family would occupy that home for an extended period, perhaps even generations; even today a very few homes after one or two centuries are still residences for descendents of their original builders. The short-term occupancy of its residents is one of the unique aspects of the Virginia Governor's House.

In the nascent days of Virginia's state government, governors were selected by the legislature and served only a one, two, or three year term. Occasional provisional governors such as James Monroe (governor from January 19, 1811 to April 3, 1811), Wyndham Robertson (governor from March 30, 1841 to March 31, 1842), and John Gregory (governor from March 31, 1842 to January 5, 1843) served a year or less. During this early period only Patrick Henry served as governor for more than one term, and at that time the capital was still seated in Williamsburg, and the governor still resided in the Governor's Palace.

Since 1852 the governor has been popularly elected, except during Reconstruction, and has served a single four year term. The Virginia Constitution does not allow a governor to succeed himself, and only one modern governor, Mills E. Godwin, Jr., was elected to a second term after being out of office for four years. In this singular instance Godwin was elected in 1965 as a Democrat and then in 1973 as a Republican.

This constant change of leaders residing in the Governor's House has had a profound impact on it, as each governor tailored its use to fit his own needs. Some, like its first occupant, James Barbour, loved to have the home open and welcomed visitors at every opportunity. It is reported that Barbour began a tradition of maintaining a supply of food and drink on the Dining Room sideboard and that he offered free

James Barbour
Courtesy Library of Virginia

entry to any legislator who wished to avail himself of this largess during the General Assembly session.[1] This open door to the punch bowl is said to have lasted until more temperate governors dried up the bowl. Governor William "Extra Billy" Smith moved the formal dining room to the basement and began to use the first floor rear parlors as one large space.

Modern governors have continued the invitations to legislators to specific receptions during sessions, and often they open the house to the general public. Stories are told of the reception hosted by Governor George Allen where so many gathered in the Ballroom that the weight of the guests on the sagging floor cut off the power in the basement. This incident was one of the most telling indications that there were significant structural problems in the building and a renovation was overdue.

Inspired by the practice of Theodore Roosevelt at the White House, Jim and I decided to open the house to anyone who wished to visit on New Year's Day, making January 1, 2000, the grand opening of the Governor's House after the major renovation which we had undertaken. With weather cooperating, on an unusual 75 degree January afternoon, Jim and I greeted thousands of guests and extended the hours of visitation until 9:00 P.M. to welcome

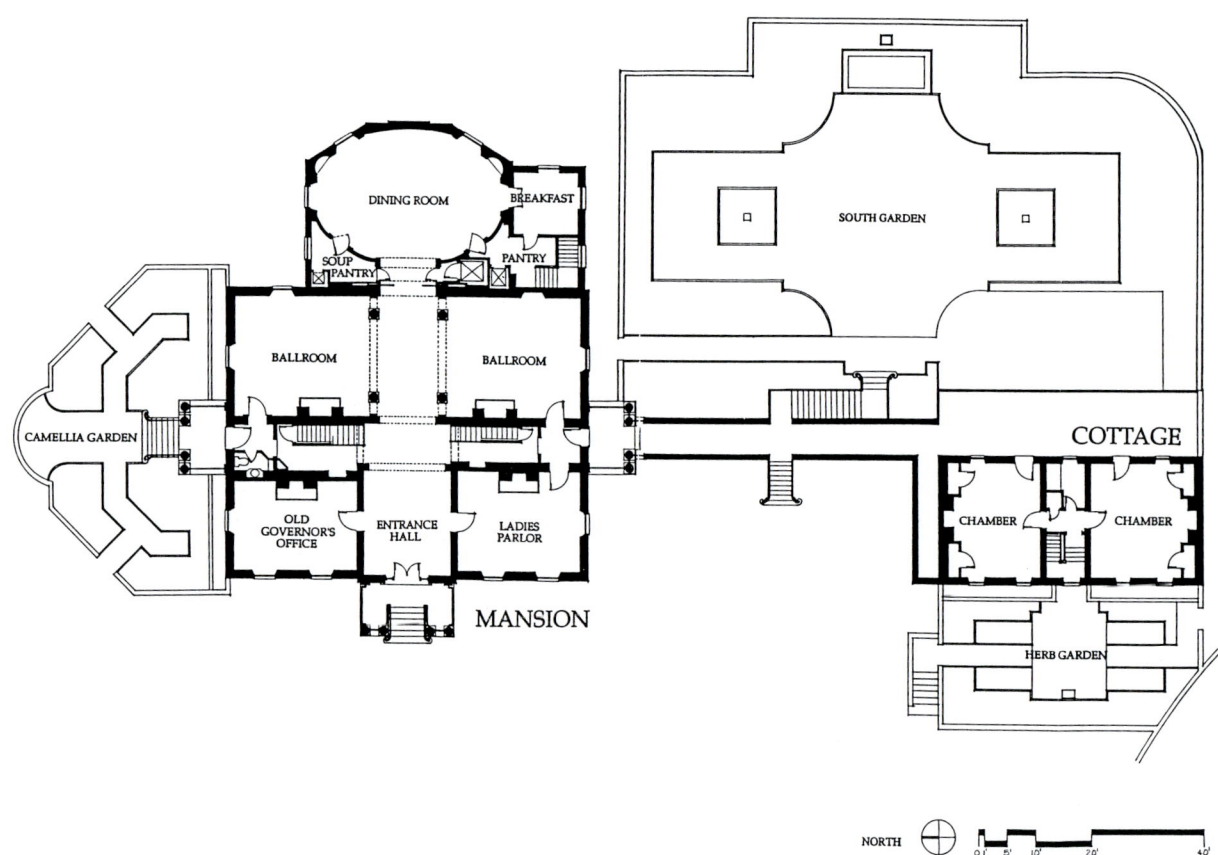

This plan shows the first floor before the 1999 renovation. The Lee changes to the rear parlors and the later Breakfast Room addition are seen. Also visible are the closed doorways of the front parlors and the lack of matching rooms flanking the Dining Room.

16   Restoring the Virginia Governor's House

many who had been standing in line for hours. The public confirmed their intense interest in the restoration project by their attendance on New Year's Day. But their interest had been ongoing during the project, with people stopping by during the day to watch the work through the fence and even make suggestions. Henry "Trev" Crider from the Department of Engineering and Buildings, tells of the person who was worried that we were taking out the original "wavy" glass and putting in plain glass panes. They had no way of knowing we were conserving the windows that were being removed and they would be returned, but nonetheless they were watching every detail. We were delighted that people wanted to watch and know what was being done. Some governors have viewed the Governor's House as more of a personal space, hosting the necessary dinners and receptions demanded by the office, but otherwise limiting public access. We believed it was the people's home as well, and we established regular visiting hours through the remainder of Jim's term.

Despite its many occupants and the differences in décor and usage they brought over the years, the House maintained a Federal style structure, and the first and second floors kept a simple four-room plan until 1906. At that time Duncan Lee, a budding architect from Ashland, Virginia, was commissioned during the Swanson administration to make significant alterations to this basic floor plan. Lee made changes to the front doorway and perhaps changed the hall ceiling plaster decorations. He removed the partition to the back parlors and opened the two rooms into the large space now called the Ballroom. He also built an addition on the rear of the house that enclosed a formal, oval Dining Room with a grand fireplace at the end of a long vista from the front door.

Though most of the Lee alterations are well-secured as part of the history of the Governor's House today, they were apparently a source of dismay for some at the time of their addition. While he was governor prior to the Lee renovations, Andrew Jackson Montague and his wife, Betsie, were unsurpassed in their interest in the decor of the House and of the focus they placed on living there from 1902 to 1906. Though the Montagues' changes might be called a "makeover" today, focusing on furnishings and beginning to move from a Victorian era décor to the then fashionable Colonial Revival, they did include repairs and changes to the building as well. It was at this time, for example, that they planned to remove Victorian era marble mantels from the Old Governor's Office and Ladies' Parlor and return the more delicate glue paste mantels original to the rooms. This change was accomplished over several administrations. The parquet of the first floor, seen in the photographs at Roosevelt's visit, was added by the Montagues as well.

After Montague left office, the major structural changes of Duncan Lee to the first floor were put into place. Though he had been out of office for eight years, Montague made his opinion of Lee's changes known in a 1914 letter to then Governor Henry Carter Stuart. Stuart was planning to make even more changes to the house by adding bedrooms over the Lee Dining Room and changing the original floor plan of the second floor to create more bedrooms and bathrooms. Though it was two terms following his governorship, Montague had maintained his interest in the House, and it surprised no one when he wrote his letter to Governor Stuart. But what Montague wrote perhaps was surprising and he leaves nothing to the imagination in his assessment of the 1906 building changes or his opinion of Stuart's proposed changes.

> I noted in the *Times Dispatch* . . . that a contract will soon be let for remodeling the Executive Mansion or the Governor's House, as originally called. My interest in this undertaking you can readily appreciate, and this interest is quickened by reason of the miser-

able abortion incident to the last improvements [of 1906], whereby the proportions of the drawing-rooms were utterly destroyed .... The new Dining Room is public, unadapted to appropriate furniture, and generally inconvenient and homely.[2]

Apparently, Montague did not approve of the large ballroom space or the oval dining area of Duncan Lee but had been unable to stop it from moving forward. Montague wrote this new letter to Stuart hoping to influence the second floor changes the governor's architect, Charles K. Bryant, was poised to make. Montague was adamant that as much as possible of the original building and its rooms be preserved and secured the support of "leading architects in the country" to support his position. "If the building is worth anything it is mainly for its historical character, and, therefore, the paramount consideration is first the retention of the building itself, and then such additions as may not impair this original structure."[3] Montague urged an addition in the area south of the House outside the old kitchen building if more space was needed upstairs, thereby eliminating structural changes to the original building in the second floor living area.

Montague's requests went unfulfilled and Stuart altered the second floor significantly. It is reported that, when Stuart moved into the House, there were three rooms upstairs along the front, with the center room traditionally serving as a nursery and the northwestern room already known as the "Lafayette Bedroom." There were also two bedrooms on the back of the house over the original rear Drawing Rooms. Stuart's changes kept the two front corner rooms but removed a wall from the nursery which was opened up creating a large room at the head of the steps now called the Capitol Room. Towards the back of the house, he kept the double door entry to the hallway which was between the two original bedrooms and now also led to two new bedrooms added over the Duncan Lee Dining Room. Stuart also replaced the old staircases with new ones that are still in use today. We found evidence of the location of the original staircases as was discussed in Chapter 1.

Though Montague had not been heeded in his suggestions about Stuart's changes at the Governor's House, he was not alone in his objections to the original Duncan Lee alterations, especially those of the main Dining Room. Governor Harry Byrd apparently agreed with Montague that there was no place along the curved walls for a sideboard, and he wanted more buffet style service to cut down on the need for staff. In 1926 Byrd had the mantled fireplace, Lee's focal point for the grand Entry Hall, removed from the center wall in the Dining Room. In the 1930s Governor James Hubert Price, echoing Montague's dismay for the large size of the Dining Room, added a porch onto the south corner where he preferred to eat. In 1958 this porch was made permanent with a two story addition which contained a formal first floor Breakfast Room and a second floor library. This addition was on the southern side of the house where Montague had earlier urged more space be sought.

In 1952 a most modern upgrade to the house was added–a central air-conditioning system. State of the art at the time, the system included metal air handlers under almost every window, covering the wainscoting in the historic areas. These units were still in use when we arrived in 1998.

The original Parris plan with these early twentieth century alterations greeted Charles and Lynda Robb when they arrived in January 1982. The Robbs modernized the second floor living quarters. They created a kitchenette and turned the double bedrooms over the Dining Room into a master bedroom suite. The House remained in this basic form until our renovation in 1998.

The exterior of the house and the other buildings on the grounds also underwent changes over the

In 1906 Duncan Lee created a long vista from the front door to the elaborate fireplace in his new Dining Room. The fireplace was removed by Governor Byrd in 1926 to create space for a sideboard to allow buffet style service.

Courtesy Library of Virginia

years. The recommendations of the original Commissioners in 1813 were gradually put into place. In 1823 a balustrade was added to the roof connecting the chimneys, and in 1830 a roofline parapet was added along with a front portico. The bricks were painted as well.

The front door was altered several times as fashions changed. An 1865 Matthew Brady photograph shows the front door as a double door with wooden panels. A photo of the 1880s shows the door had been replaced with one that had glass panels, popular in the late Victorian age. Perhaps the door was changed when the balustrade, parapet and panels were removed after the Civil War due to their dilapidated condition. There was concern in the diminished economic conditions following the war about the cost of maintaining these features and the decision was made to remove them to conserve money. In 1989 during the Baliles administration the changes that had been made after the Civil War for economy were reversed. The balustrade, parapet and panels were returned, and the 1830 appearance was restored.

In 1835, again following the suggestion of the original Commissioners, the grounds were filled in and a coach house and stable were built to replace the original stable of 1792, which was torn down. The later structure was eventually replaced by the current Carriage House.

Matthew Brady photographed this image of the house in 1865. The 1830s parapet, balustrade and panels were still in place as were the double, wooden paneled front doors.

Courtesy Valentine Richmond History Center

By the 1880's the parapet, balustrade and panels had been removed due to the cost of maintaining them and a change in fashion. The front door was now a Victorian style glass door with a glass transom and side panels.

Courtesy The Cook Collection, Valentine Richmond History Center

In 1846 the Governor's House and Kitchen were connected by the covered passage that still exists today. This was during the changes of Governor "Extra Billy" Smith when more focus was placed on the use of the basement for dining. Vouchers for building materials supplied in 1846 indicate that the passage was covered with latticework, probably to shade the frequently used area from the strong morning sun. At some later time the passage was enclosed and it was extensively altered during the 1955 work that

Governor Stanley did in the garden, including the addition of an iron railing and steps. The brick wall that completely encircles the grounds today was built in 1955. A guard house was added at the entrance of this wall in 1961 at the request of First Lady Josephine Almond who was concerned about the guards who had to stand watch in the elements.

These ongoing changes by those in residence at the Governor's House loomed large over our commitment to save this historic structure. As we began our investigation about how to proceed with our restoration, almost a century after Governor Montague's letter to Stuart, his words still seemed to echo through the halls to us: "If the building is worth anything it is mainly for its historical character, and, therefore, the paramount consideration is first the retention of the building itself, and then such additions as may not impair this original structure." In 1998 the team we assembled to do our complete restoration of the House undertook an extensive examination of the building and of adaptations needed for modern living. We made a commitment to save as much as possible of the original building, and we made accommodations for modern systems in a building addition. In many ways Montague's vision was finally fulfilled.

In 1961 a small guardhouse was added to the 1954 brick wall surrounding the grounds. Despite objections from some who thought it detracted from the appearance of the house, Josephine Almond insisted that it be built to protect the Capitol Policemen who stood guard at the entrance.

Courtesy Library of Virginia

A plaque on the front wall near the guardhouse commemorates the restoration project and the committee that oversaw it.

Photography by Scott Tumperi

CHAPTER 3

Defining the Project and Assembling the Team

Anyone who has been involved in a home renovation, whether it is a new kitchen or just re-wallpapering a room, can attest to the myriad details that must be addressed at all phases of the project. When the home is a historic structure, the issues in the project increase almost exponentially. When the home is the Governor's House, they are not only countless in number, but they are scrutinized by countless people. Compounding the details that have to be addressed is the short length of time that any governor has to live there. Because Virginia's Constitution that says that a governor cannot succeed himself, a governor has only one term–four years in office. The legislature is already in session at the time a new governor is inaugurated, and he must pay full attention from the start of the session or he loses an entire legislative period. Moreover, it takes time to acclimate one's family to life in Capitol Square, and the countless receptions that are held at the house while the Assembly is in Richmond can skew one's view of what life is really like.

All of these factors led to years of deferring much needed structural work on the Governor's House, though most modern administrations had taken on some individual projects. Issues of inadequate furnishings and a desire to include appropriate period antique furnishings were addressed by First Lady Virginia Rogers "Jinks" Holton, who created the Citizens Advisory Committee in 1973. This group had a charge to assemble Federal and Colonial Revival antiques for the historic first floor. Her efforts were followed by Katherine Godwin and Edwina "Eddy" Dalton, who both worked to collect even more period pieces, some of which were still in the House in 1998. At the end of his administration, John Dalton asked the

General Assembly to appropriate funds to address the growing structural and mechanical problems. Funds were appropriated at the end of his term.

As Charles and Lynda Robb moved into the Governor's House in 1982 they used these funds and some left from his inauguration to address issues, room by room, mostly in the living quarters. They fixed the Heating, Ventilation, and Air-conditioning (HVAC) system and made changes to the second floor. Lynda Robb recalls that the governor's bedroom was the smallest in the house, with four doors and a window with an air-conditioning unit. Only a double bed would fit. The bathroom would flood, and there was nowhere to dine or keep food. Addressing each of these issues one by one and hiring a contractor from Winchester, the Robbs converted the two small bedrooms created by Governor Stuart over the Dining Room into a bedroom suite, fixed a Dining Room upstairs, and converted the governor's shower to a pantry with a refrigerator. This basic floor plan existed when we arrived.

Structural concerns of the house exterior and a return to its Federal exterior décor were undertaken during the administration of Gerald Baliles. The 175th anniversary of the Governor's House was celebrated in 1988, and in 1989 the house was returned to its 1830s exterior appearance. As Parris originally designed the house its exterior was fairly plain. A sketch by Parris showed the completed house without decorative panels, balustrade, or roofline parapet. The balustrades, parapets and decorative panels, added to the house by 1830 and removed after the Civil War because of the expense to maintain them, were all returned and the porches repaired in the 1989 project.

Governor Douglas Wilder worked to make the fireplaces wood burning and to make sure the chimneys were in sound condition. Exhaust fans were installed to help the chimneys draw properly. Wilder also replaced the wood floors in the living quarters. In 1992 the first attempt to make the house accessible was made with the installation of the handicap lift at the west garden wall. Also, attempts were made to repaint and restore the hand-painted Gracie wallpaper in the Breakfast Room on the first floor.

As Governor in 1994 George Allen paid additional attention to household furnishings. A complete set of dining room chairs was commissioned and a Stark carpet was specially designed for the Dining Room.

Second floor plan

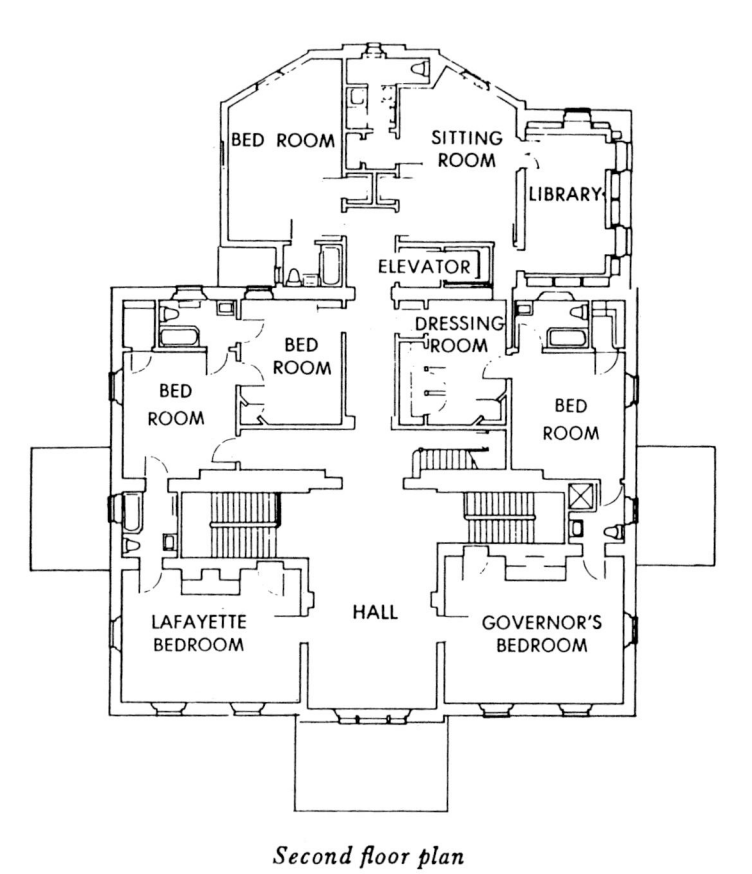

The Robbs found this second floor plan on their arrival. They reconfigured the bedroom and sitting room into one large room with a bathroom on the side. They converted the bathroom adjacent to the Governor's Bedroom into a kitchenette.

24 Restoring the Virginia Governor's House

LEFT: *Workmen replace the parapet and balustrade during the Baliles administration.*
Courtesy Richmond Times-Dispatch Collection, Valentine Richmond History Center
RIGHT: *Specially designed carpet, draperies and shield back dining room chairs were commissioned during the Allen administration.*
Courtesy DHR

New draperies completed the decoration of this much used area.

While numerous needs such as these were addressed during the decades of the 80s and 90s, major structural issues were not addressed, leading to the poor general condition of the Governor's House on the eve of the Gilmore administration in 1998.

In the weeks preceding Jim's inauguration, the Director of the Department of General Services, Donald C. Williams, and the Director of the Division of Engineering and Buildings, Nathan "Irv" Broocke, approached the Gilmore transition team and discussed the need for extensive work at the residence. They asked the new Secretary of Administration, G. Bryan Slater, to discuss the project with Governor-elect Gilmore. This was not the first trip those in General Services had made to request that a governor undertake the massive project, but their pleas had never been answered. The General Assembly had already recognized the need for an undertaking of this scope at the Governor's House, and they had already voted to fund a full restoration project for the house. But no administration had been willing to accept the obligation, the inconvenience, or the scrutiny that a project with the scope of the renovation would incur.

Williams and Broocke laid out the details and urgency of the project and indicated that it would require the family to be out of the house for at least a year. As other governors had before, Jim hesitated at this part of the request, but unlike others he made a counter-offer. While serving as Attorney General, Jim had become aware of the appropriation for work at the Governor's House, so the request had not come as a surprise. In his vast reading he had learned about the renovation of the White House by Harry Truman and had seen the widely publicized photo of the bulldozer in the middle of the White House. Convinced by the request that the needs of the residence were real, Jim offered for our family to vacate the house for six months. He told General Services that if the Navy could refit the aircraft carrier Yorktown in 48 hours and get it out to Midway, then surely with proper planning and attention the Governor's House could be restored in six months. He also believed that placing a time limit would require that the team maintain proper planning methods and would give the project a focus which would prevent it from ballooning into an unending building disaster.

Though nervous about the prospect of completing an undertaking of this size in six months, Williams and Broocke realized that this was probably the best offer they would ever get and they took it, immediately wondering how they would accomplish this Herculean task. But wonder quickly became action, and Williams and Broocke began to coordinate with Secretary of Administration Slater to put together a team to oversee the restoration effort. I was among those contacted.

On April 24, 1998, Donald Williams asked me to be the Chairman of the Executive Committee of the renovation. The agenda for our meeting included not only a review of the scope and a status report of the project to date, but lists of "Next Steps" that included projected deadlines and committees with proposed members. It was clear that the Department of General Services had thought the process through completely and had taken the Governor's time limit to heart. I agreed to the role of chairman with the understanding that this would be a working effort and not just the use of my name. I also said that the mission should be a historic restoration as much as possible; I believed that on the first floor all decisions should be based on historic research and that even questions of décor should be made with historic findings as a guide. I hoped this would end the "revolving door" décor changes on the first floor and make the house the historic treasure it should be.

The remainder of the Executive and Building Committees that were assembled were composed of representatives from the Executive and Legislative branches. From the Executive branch were logical departments to participate in a project of this scope– Secretariat of Administration: Secretary G. Bryan Slater,

Alex B. Oliver of Williamsburg worked to give the Citizens Advisory Committee (CAC) by-laws and an up-to-date house inventory. The committee was regularly informed about the progress of the renovation. Courtesy DHR

26 Restoring the Virginia Governor's House

Deputy Secretary Donald L. Moseley, L. William Reid, Jr.; Department of Historic Resources: Director H. Alexander Wise, Jr., William M. Crosby, and Cara Metz; Executive Mansion: Director Donna P. Case, Chef Mark W. Herndon, Martin "Tutti" Townes, First Sergeant Ronald M. Watkins; Department of General Services: Director Donald C. Williams, Deputy Director Demerst B. Smit, Deputy Director William G. Poston; and Division of Engineering and Buildings: Director Nathan I. Broocke, Bruce E. Brooks, Henry G. Shirley, John F. Mitchell, Jr., Henry T. Crider, Jr., and Anthony C. Griffin, Jr. Each of these members brought special expertise to the project that would address multiple systems and needs. Also included on the Building Committee were representatives from both the Senate and the House of Delegates. Senator Benjamin J. Lambert, III and Delegate Vincent F. Callahan, Jr. both readily agreed to participate and help coordinate this public-private project.

The first meetings of the committee involved defining the scope of the project, planning a course of action, and creating a timeline for its completion. The multitude of problems that had beset the structure gave little doubt that all systems–HVAC, electrical, and plumbing–would need complete renovation. Whether this would be done as a historic renovation or just a project that would address fixing these systems in any way possible was one our first questions.

One of the foremost problems was that the house was not designed for modern living, so upgrading the worn-out systems without removing significant original building structure would be difficult. There was mixed discussion over the direction the project would take, and so I suggested that we tour the historically restored Wickham House which, like the Governor's House, had been designed by Alexander Parris. The Wickham House had just completed a major restoration, and while

This house of Richmond businessman John Wickham was designed by Alexander Parris during the same period that Parris designed the Governor's House. The restoration of this structure was an important source of information for the Governor's House restoration.
Courtesy Valentine Richmond History Center

their needs were not exactly like the Governor's House (since The Wickham House is no longer a residence) nonetheless, some issues and methods of construction would be consistent and provide helpful guidance. By making such a visit, the committee could get a good understanding of the extent of historic restoration possible on the Governor's House and better determine the demands that they would face.

At the invitation of William Martin, director of the Valentine Museum (now the Richmond History Center), the committee spent an afternoon touring the Wickham House from first floor to attic, analyzing

Defining the Project and Assembling the Team 27

the special requirements of a historic renovation. After this tour we committed to proceed as a *historic* project and assembled the construction and architectural teams. Martin and his staff became valuable sources of information about Alexander Parris and period houses and furnishings; they were always willing to share what they had learned during their project, as were the staffs of other historic houses across the Commonwealth.

The executive management team later agreed that in addition to deciding the historic scope of the project, perhaps the most critical early decision the team made was to hire the Construction Manager (CM) first, then engage the CM in the selection process of the architectural team and require the CM be on site at all times during the project. The selection of the CM and placing the "CM at risk" was the first time the Department of General Services had used this project method instead of the normal state bidding procedure. But the result of this variation was the creation of a team approach to the efforts that ensured everyone was working together. *This became the key to the success of the project.*

Examination of the selection process of the Construction Manager shows the focus and efficiency of the Building Team. Seven firms made submittals to be considered for pre-qualification to be interviewed, and on April 20, 1998, all seven were asked to submit a proposal. Each was asked to attend a mandatory pre-proposal conference and tour the Governor's House on April 27. Final proposals from the firms were due to the committee on May 1, 4 days later. On May 8 the committee's review of these proposals was complete, and the building committee met to review and rank the proposals on May 11. From May 11 through May 15 separate interviews were held in the General Assembly Building with each firm.

Ultimately Daniel and Company, Inc. (DCI) led by Sam Daniel, General Contractor, and Michael Westcott, Project Manager, of Richmond, was chosen as the construction firm. Lewis Nuckols and Robbie Bliley would be the Project Superintendents for DCI at the jobsite. Gloria Alley was stationed in the office trailer to keep the administrative details under control. A second interview process was then undertaken to find the best architectural firm to add to the team. Hanbury, Evans, Newill and Vlattas and Company (HENV) of Norfolk, Virginia, led by John Paul Hanbury, architect, and Barbara Strickland-Page, interior design specialist, was chosen as the design firm. In addition to providing the soundest economic proposals, each of these firms had extensive experience in historic renovations, including other projects in Capitol Square. Daniel and Company had been the project manager for the exterior renovation of the Governor's House in 1989; Hanbury Evans had worked on interior projects at the Capitol Building, including the third floor, which houses the Governor's office.

LEFT TO RIGHT: *John Paul Hanbury, architect, Sam Daniel, general contractor and Mike Westcott, project manager worked closely together for a successful project.*
Courtesy DHR

To carry out the plans and directives of the construction and architectural team, we selected the engineering firms of Cherwa-Ewing Engineering, P.C., McPherson and Associates, P.C., and Austin Brockenbrough and Associates, L.L.P. through a similar bidding process.

Assembling an experienced team was arguably the most significant task we accomplished during the project because of all the decisions they would make, but it would take more than experience for the various teams of people who would have to work together to be successful. It would take a belief that bringing the project as we had defined it to a successful conclusion was really all that mattered and would be reward for all. Reflecting on this, Donald Williams of the Department of General Services said he thought that passion was the element that all members of the team possessed, and that it was that drive that kept everyone focused on the end goal, helped them ignore comments like "is that really what you want to do, fix that old house?" and got them over the inevitable surprise structural problems that arose. There is no question that everyone involved in the renovation put the success of the project first. The sign at the entrance to the house in all caps – SCHEDULE – SCHEDULE – SCHEDULE – became not a burden, but a mantra for success. Everyone attended the regular meetings of the team and provided or found necessary technical information immediately, so that quick–but *informed*–decisions were made when problems arose.

The notice SCHEDULE, SCHEDULE, SCHEDULE was an ever-present reminder to workmen of how critical on-time completion of the project was.

Courtesy DHR

Critical to making the appropriate decisions involving the historic integrity of the building was the attention devoted to the restoration by the Department of Historic Resources (DHR). DHR, headed by H. Alexander Wise and represented at the team meetings by William M. Crosby, was always on hand to promptly evaluate construction issues vis-à-vis the historic fabric of the house and ensure that the history of the building remained a primary focus.

As well as providing historic analyses, DHR made the commitment to document the entire project through a photographic and video record. They hired Sadler and Whitehead, Architects, PLC, to photograph each day's work throughout the entire project. Still photographs and video images were taken by Mary Harding Sadler and Joseph D. Lahendro, and their efforts are available on the Library of Virginia website. Detailed descriptions of the work are included for each day, and many of their photos are included here.

Two final groups were also critical to the completion of the project. The Citizens Advisory Committee for the Executive Mansion (CAC) and The Foundation for the Preservation of the Executive Mansion were keys to success. Created in 1973 and comprised of individuals appointed for four-year terms by the Governor, the CAC had as its job the acquisition of furnishings, both new and antique, authorizing repairs of existing pieces and de-accessioning pieces that were no longer of value. The CAC was created during the administration of Governor Linwood Holton when there was a major move to obtain furnishings appropriate to a historic residence like the Governor's House. However, prior to the Gilmore restoration the CAC had no bylaws and no set policy for accepting donations or deciding what was no longer needed. On our arrival we found that some furnishings listed as having been at the Governor's House were no longer there and that there was no record of what had happened to them. Some pieces were said to be on loan to universities and colleges, but there were no records of what pieces had been loaned or which institution had them. Under the leadership of Alex B. Oliver, the Chairman of the CAC during the restoration, a search was undertaken to try to find as many pieces as possible, bylaws were written that required the creation of an inventory, and rules were put into place that governed the accession and de-accession of furnishings.

Though it had accepted donations of furniture and art for years, the CAC had no real authority to request funds from the legislature or raise funds for purchases such as draperies or carpets. To address this issue we created The Foundation for the Preservation of the Executive Mansion and asked Joseph Ferrell of Richmond to chair the effort to raise funds for non-building related expenses of the Governor's House restoration. Document drapery fabrics, carpets, and wall coverings are expensive items in historic restoration. State funds were appropriated only for the structural and systems needs of the house. The new Foundation raised and reported all the funds required for the decorative purchases of the project. Contributions to The Foundation also made it possible to upgrade system changes from the basic items that state appropriations covered. John Gioia of Fairfax, for example, wanted to make the house a "smart house," with the latest technology and the ability to easily upgrade the technological systems as advances were made. With the Foundation in place he was able to make a contribution to ensure that such an upgrade could be put in place.

The restoration of the Governor's House is a true example of what can happen when a team works together and places its whole focus on the task at hand. In the end, it was all of the planning, enthusiastic participation and, most of all, passion that allowed the restoration of the Governor's House to be finished on time and under budget, outcomes as commendable as the work itself. But this really should come as no surprise, because the story of those who have taken care of the house for two centuries is one of working together. Living in the Mansion for the first year made it clear to me how critical the proposed work on the house was. But what was just as clear was how hard everyone had worked for years–from the Department of General Services, to the House staff, to the Executive Protection Unit (EPU), to the Grounds Crew–to keep the House comfortable, safe, and a place to be proud of, not only for the families who live there, but for all of those who visit.

CHAPTER 4

Where We Started— Governor Tyler Would Have Felt At Home

By 1998 the Executive Mansion had reached a condition that must have been similar to that when Governor Tyler declared the first Richmond Governor's House unsuitable for habitation in 1811. When we moved the Gilmore family into the building in January, it did not take long to encounter the variety of problems that had beset this structure. Many were obvious and well-known; others were more subtle and hidden by the elegant décor, or were in areas not seen by the public.

Not designed for modern living, every major system of the house–electrical, HVAC, and plumbing–had serious flaws. The electrical system was a tangle of wires, so complicated that a coffee maker in the basement of the house affected the operation of the Governor's computer on the third floor. Access to cable and computer was through a random maze of wiring.

It took only one spring and summer to recognize the shortcomings of the HVAC system. It was

Metal air handlers were under every window on the first floor. They condensed moisture which rotted the wainscot behind and stained the floors and carpets. Courtesy DHR

amazing that any system could be so ineffective and destructive; the damage that had been done to historic features was irreparable in some places. The air-conditioning system looked like every 1950s Sunday school building. Painted metal air-handlers were under every window in the house, impossible to disguise and because of their age equally inadequate in their cooling task. Each register condensed moisture as it struggled unsuccessfully to cool; this moisture dripped constantly on the parquet flooring, staining or rotting the wood. On extremely hot days rivulets of water reached the Stark carpet which had been specially loomed for the Dining Room, staining it irreversibly. The moisture also attacked the wainscoting behind the air-handlers. When the first of these was removed, we saw extensive, often permanent, water damage to the paneling, requiring complete replacement.

The plumbing also had created some of the more visible problems. The north Ballroom ceiling had a permanent stain from leaky pipes in an upstairs bathroom. Above this stain was our son Ashton's bathtub. When the second-floor flooring was removed during the demolition phase of the project, in addition to leaky pipes they found that the joists encasing the tub were not reattached after being cut to add the tub. We were fortunate that Ashton did not arrive at a reception one evening via his bathtub!

The unattached joists in this bathroom were only one example of the numerous additions to the already lengthy list of structural problems revealed during the planning phase. When the 1813 rear parlors of the Parris-designed first floor were combined by Duncan Lee into one large space to create the Ballroom, the broad expanse of open floor invited large groups to congregate in this open space. Time had weakened the supports for the ballroom area, and they were no longer able to support the heavy weights of these large crowds. The weakened state of the Ballroom floor supports had been perfectly known ever since a reveal-

LEFT: *Though shiny and clean, this tub was discovered to be unsecured in the floor.* Courtesy DHR
RIGHT: *The original wooden peg supports for the first floor fireplaces were found in the basement ceilings.*
Courtesy DHR

ing episode during the administration of George Allen. So many people crowded into the center of the Ballroom that the deflection of the floor turned off the power in the basement!

Historic precedent exists for having a Capitol Square structure collapse–the balcony in the old House Chamber of the Capitol collapsed in April 1870 from overcrowding on inadequate supports. At the time, the chamber was being used as a Court of Appeals, and hundreds of people had crowded in to see a case of local interest. More than fifty people were killed in the tragedy which probably was caused by improper installation of the balcony's beams. Not wishing to have history repeat itself in the Governor's House, crowd size was limited to 150 after the Allen incident in the Ballroom.

One of the biggest surprises for me, however, came one day as I was preparing to leave for school. I had gotten the rest of the family off for the day and entered the small, one-person elevator to go from the living quarters down to the basement to meet the Executive Protection Unit (EPU) to head out

Duncan Lee's use of so many of Parris' elements such as the arch and classical frieze, made it important to consider both architects, especially in the Entry Hall.

Courtesy DHR

for the day. While going down, I heard what sounded like a shower running and wondered who that could possibly be since I was the only one still at home. When I got to the Kitchen, I asked the butler, Martin "Tutti" Townes, if he knew anything about the running water. Tutti assured me that everything was all right and that it was just raining outside. When I asked what that had to do with the elevator, Tutti replied, "Well, the elevator just fills with water when it rains." He proceeded to go into the old Laundry Room where the works of the elevator were in a closet. He manually raised the elevator into the shaft so that when the doors were opened, we could see down into the well of the elevator. Much to my amazement the shaft was indeed filling with water. From that moment on I never had another thought of turning back in the plans to renovate the Governor's House.

Deciding that the structure needed repair was the easy part. However, the historic nature of the Governor's House complicated plans to upgrade the building's systems and structure. The arch decorations from the 1813 Parris design, the original plaster frieze, and the 1906 ceiling medallion of Duncan Lee still adorned the first floor entry; parquet flooring installed in 1903 by Governor Montague covered the floors. There was no discussion of removing these features to get to wiring or plumbing because the delicate features would have been destroyed in the process. Primary installation of systems, wiring or plumbing, or structural reinforcements to the first floor would have to be done underneath the floors or above the ceilings in order to preserve these historic elements. Over the life of the building both the basement and second floor had been altered extensively so access through those spaces was possible because of the

The House Director's office not only had low ceilings but exposed pipes and beams.
Courtesy DHR

reduced amount of historic building structure left in those areas.

While the numerous prior alterations to the basement and second floor would give access to the first floor, these same alterations had also created unique renovation needs for those two floors. The basement was a perplexing maze of rooms that existed on different levels. There was a large height difference throughout the floor and eventually the floor had to be excavated to a depth of four feet in the EPU's office to get it on a level with the rest of the basement. As it was, ceilings in that area had been quite low, and in the EPU office they were so low that some of the state troopers had difficulty standing up straight. Because of the steps and multiple levels there was no wheelchair access possible in the basement. Throughout the basement storage rooms were inconsistent in size. Some were tiny, and some of these very small areas served double duty as storage and staff offices; other rooms were overly large and wasted much needed space.

In addition to the inconvenience of this basement floor, an antiquated, inadequate Kitchen was housed here. A walk-in refrigerator hardly cooled enough to serve as a flower box. Two residential dishwashers strained to accommodate large dinner parties and receptions, and a four-burner, electric stove took forever to heat large pots of water or anything else. The staff joked that if Chef Mark Herndon required a big pot of hot water, he would phone someone at the Governor's House before he left home in Williamsburg and tell them to put the pot on to boil. By the time he drove the one hour from home, the water would be hot. Once hot, though, the burners took forever to cool making it almost impossible to cook anything that required temperature control. It was a kitchen hardly equipped for the entertaining that is done there, and its access to the rest of the house was challenging.

Food for entertaining or for the family had to be carried from the basement to the upper floors using either stairs at the rear of the Kitchen to the first floor, a small dumbwaiter that was at the rear of the Kitchen and opened into a small anteroom off of the Breakfast Room, or the antiquated small elevator that serviced all floors. The elevator had the most significant problems. First, it was small, providing enough space for only one rider; two could squeeze in for a very up close and per-

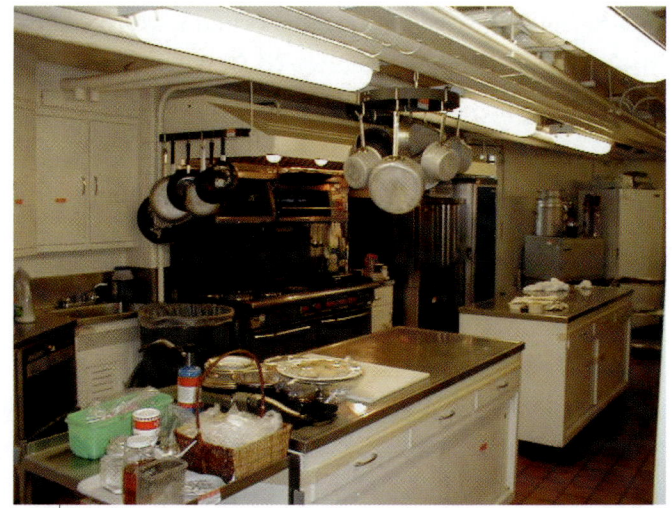

The Kitchen work area had exposed pipes and lighting. Its electric stove was difficult to manage.
Courtesy Library of Virginia

34 Restoring the Virginia Governor's House

LEFT: *In the living quarters, a walk-through kitchenette had a stove that did not work and no oven.* RIGHT: *The governor's bathroom was small and had a toilet that frequently overflowed.*

Courtesy DHR

sonal trip. Second, the elevator itself was outdated, and parts needed to keep it in service were no longer manufactured. Spare parts from other elevators being taken out of service were purchased to keep just in case they were needed at the Governor's House. Finally, the elevator's location next to the pocket door that separated the Ballroom and Dining Room meant that if the shaft were to be enlarged for wheel-chair access, the arched entry to the Dining Room would have to be removed. This was a major history versus modern living question we would have to address. And these problems were all in addition to the fact that the elevator shaft filled with water when it rained!

The second floor of the house presented problems similar to those in the basement. The private living quarters on this floor rambled like the basement; it was like a rabbit warren that led from one small room to an attached smaller room. The large, historically maintained Lafayette Bedroom was connected to a small bedroom in the family quarters by a bathroom which was intended to serve both bedrooms. That small bedroom opened into a long hallway that led back into the main hallway, into an adjoining small bedroom, and into another bathroom.

Off of the main hall, the governor's Dressing Room also had multiple doorways. Not only did it have the door to the hall, but there was a rear door into a room that had been used as a dining room, a door into his bathroom, and a door to a hall-like area that entered either the library or his bedroom. All of these doors made the Governor's Dressing Room one of the most direct routes from room to room on the south side of the second floor, thus giving little privacy in this space. And there were closet doors as well as all of the others!

The paneled den could only be reached through the governor's bedroom or Dressing Room. This location made using it to host guests difficult.
Courtesy DHR

One of the most beautiful rooms on the second floor was the richly paneled library that had been added in 1954. This room overlooked the garden and had the potential of being one of the most used rooms of the house. In fact, Governor Allen occasionally used the library for cabinet meetings. But getting to this room was difficult since its only access was through the Governor's bedroom or his Dressing Room.

In addition to its inconvenient layout, much of the second floor was in a state of disrepair and lacked basic living features for any family. The governor's bathroom was extremely small, with only a tiny shower stall, a toilet and a sink. The plumbing here had frequent problems. In the small area that had been designated as a kitchen, it was impossible to bake cookies or prepare anything more than tea. It was truly only a kitchenette with a small refrigerator, and a stove with two burners. There was no hood for cooking, nor was there an oven for baking. It was better than

A Christmas tree fire in 1926 that trapped family members on the second floor led to making fire safety a priority. It was one of the main considerations during the renovation.
Courtesy Library of Virginia

36 Restoring the Virginia Governor's House

the reported "toaster oven on a toilet" that was rumored to have existed for one governor's family, but only marginally.

Fire suppression and emergency exits were always issues for the first family and were a major concern of the EPU, especially on the second floor. The only exits from the second floor were the two staircases going down into the front hall and the antiquated elevator in the back of the house. They worried about the potential of another fire like the one that occurred at the end of the Christmas holiday in 1925. A personal account of a long-time House staff member gives a chilling account of the tragedy when on January 4, 1926, a fire, which had started in the dried out Christmas tree, swept through the house.

> I ran into the Mansion, and saw the left side of the Ballroom in a regular mass of flames. I set out the alarm and did all I could. In the meantime, Lee Trinkle, who was 13 years old, was the only member of the family upstairs. Everyone else got out, but he was trapped in the south back bedroom, and when we got the Mansion's only tall ladder set up against the back of the house to get him, we saw the ladder was broken. Mrs. Trinkle got in a panic for the safety of her son and rushed up the burning staircase to his room. She was very badly burnt; the stairs were a mass of flames. Then the firemen came and threw up a ladder to the bedroom window, and got her out. Young Lee Trinkle jumped and wasn't hurt at all, but Mrs. Trinkle was taken to the Memorial Hospital where she stayed for a long time. The governor got a room next to her, and they never came back to the Mansion to sleep again.[1]

To try to prevent such a situation from happening again, residential smoke detectors were placed throughout the house and rope ladders were kept at various windows on the second floor. But even some of these were inadequate. Shortly after moving in I was examining the rooms with Donna Case, the House Director. We discovered that a rope ladder to be used in case of fire had been placed in a blanket chest. But everyone was dismayed when we realized that the rope wasn't tied to anything, and if it were tied to something it wasn't long enough even to reach the window, much less the ground. It could have been much like the broken ladder that had confronted the staff during the 1926 fire.

LEFT: *Before the renovation Jim set up a personal office in the southwest corner room of the second floor.* RIGHT: *Often we took family meals in what we were now calling the Capitol Room because of its view of Capitol Square.*

Courtesy DHR

Despite their shortcomings, these were the living quarters that would serve our family until the major project could be undertaken. Until that time choices had to be made about how rooms on the third floor would be used for the beginning of the administration. Using some furniture that we had brought from our library at home, Jim set up an office in the southwest room of the second floor. It was near the head of the stairs and if the double doors were closed to the back of the house it did not infringe too much on our privacy in the back.

If I were to have any chance to have office space, it would have to be in the area between the kitchenette and governor's Dressing Room that had been used by other families as a dining room; I set up this space as an office, and since there was really no need to use the door into his Dressing Room, that door remained closed.

For dining, we placed a round table in front of the large window in the room at the head of the steps that overlooks Capitol Square. This area came to be called the Capitol Room, and most of our family dining was done there if we didn't go downstairs to the Breakfast Room. Though this new dining arrangement might seem to have lacked privacy because of the daily tours that gathered right at the foot of the steps and went throughout the first floor, the area was much brighter and more open than the cramped little room that had served as a dining room. The Capitol Room also has a lovely view of the Capitol, and we found it pleasurable to dine there. Tutti could bring meals down the main hall without going through Jim's dressing room. And in the end, tours did not matter at all since the house closed over the lunch hour from noon until two every afternoon.

Like the other families who had lived in the Governor's House before us, we made accommodations that allowed us to live reasonably comfortably despite growing knowledge of the deterioration of the house. Though the notorious and visible problems in the house–many of them safety related– had sealed our decision to renovate, the Building Committee did not want to encounter unknown problems that would stop progress once our family moved out and construction started. We decided to undertake an eighteen month pre-construction phase of investigations while we were still in residence to finalize the scope that the restoration would take, hopefully completing the list of difficulties that would have to be addressed during construction.

This decision proved fortuitous because discoveries and decisions based on them completely altered the scope of the project as it was originally conceived. It was at this time that we decided to include renovations to the Carriage House and Cottage. We also concluded that an addition on the northeast corner of the Governor's House was the best way to make it handicap accessible without destroying large amounts of the historic structure of the building.

Most significantly, these pre-construction efforts prevented a major problem that we discovered at this time from being left unaddressed completely, leaving the building unsafe, or completely derailing the whole schedule of the project. Houses built during the time of the Governor's House were generally constructed with no footings as we use today, but were begun by just laying bricks for the walls on the bare ground in a foundation trench. To examine the integrity of the lowest bricks, test borings were made of the lower levels of the walls to verify their stability. These tests revealed that two of the four walls were eroded in the lowest courses of brick, and they were crumbling and in critical need of repair. In the Director's office, Donna Case admits to being nervous coming to work when we found that the foundation of the wall in her office reminded us of cookie crumbs. This was the most significant hidden problem discovered during the testing phase and was exactly the type of issue we were trying to determine.

In addition to identifying needed corrections to the structure, the pre-construction phase of the project allowed us to make decisions that prevented redundancies in systems and thus hold costs in line. Hot water and heat for the Governor's House are generated at the steam plant at the Medical College of Virginia. Back-up heating for the residence would be an unnecessary investment because upgrades were already being made at the MCV steam plant as well as in the distribution lines.

All of this planning was essential to completing everything within six months. If we had not known all of these needs before construction began, unforeseen twists such as a new building addition, and problems of the magnitude of the eroded foundation, would have thrown the renovation hopelessly behind from the very first hammer blow.

Living in the Governor's House for the first year made it clear to me how critical the proposed work on the house was. There were genuine safety problems, there were much needed upgrades to systems, and there were basic issues of livability. I had also come to appreciate the history that had been made here over the years and the role this building had played in those events. But what was even clearer now was how hard everyone had worked for years–from the Department of General Services, to the House staff, to the EPU, to the Grounds Crew–to keep the House as comfortable and safe as possible for its residents and guests. That had been no small task, and their efforts are much appreciated.

Modern conservation methods including the use of x-ray and infrared photography discovered that the Queen Elizabeth portrait had been extensively altered at some earlier time. A landscape backed portrait with a new hair style, crown and lost cross emerged after extensive work that removed over-paint and grime. An article written by Tracy Kamerer explaining the finds can be found in the Spring 2002 issue of Virginia Cavalcade.

Courtesy Library of Virginia

CHAPTER 5

Using Technology to Gather Historical Data

*I*n addition to searching for structural and mechanical information during the renovation pre-construction phase, as much historical data as could be found were collected about the Governor's House and about houses and furnishings of the period. Maintaining the historical integrity of the structure was a top priority, and the project was a *restoration* as much as a *renovation*. One of the first realizations of the difference in the scope of a restoration and a renovation came when the committee seemed reluctant to accept the necessity of maintaining as much of the original framework of the structure as possible when adding new systems.

Our visit to the Wickham House had illustrated to those who had not been previously involved in a historic building project the importance of salvaging historic building fabric, as well as the possibility that it could be done. Because the Wickham House is a museum and is no longer used as a residence, the needs there were sometimes different than those we required at the Governor's House, and certain methods employed in their restoration project could not be incorporated in our project. Their fire suppression system, for example, uses a halon gas system which smothers the fire by robbing the atmosphere of oxygen needed to burn. Obviously this is not an appropriate system for a residence/office like the Governor's House because of the numbers of people present at most times. Nonetheless, their preservation of original building fabric in adding such a system was similar to the issues present in our project and was instructional for those on the tour.

Historical information about the appearance of the Governor's House was researched in various ways

Frank Welsh spent hours examining microscopic views of paint chips to reveal paint colors and evidence of wall coverings. His efforts determined the original colors of the walls and mantels, the faux finishing of the doors, and whether baseboards and column bases had been marbleized.

Courtesy DHR

other than consulting with the Valentine Museum. Frank Welsh, an architectural coatings consultant from Bryn Mawr, Pennsylvania, conducted microscopic paint research that told a great deal about the original appearance of the front parlors and hall. Though vouchers are still on file at the Library of Virginia from the earliest years of the Governor's House, the bills are not specific as to colors and patterns of paint or Brussels carpeting that were purchased. Welsh took tiny chips of wall surface from many areas—walls, sills, mantels, ceilings, window frames, and other areas that had been painted—throughout the house and examined them under the microscope. This and chemical analysis gave a glimpse at the paint that had been added over the years. These layers and paint types helped give a date range for the colors and methods of application.

Welsh's analysis showed us that the earliest paint color on the wainscoting of the parlors and hallway was gray. The mantels were painted gray as well. The baseboards, tops of chair rails, and mantel tops were a chocolate brown. His research also found the first primary evidence, from 1813, that the doors were faux-finished, wood-grained mahogany. The ghosts of box locks, found when the paint was stripped away during conservation, told us even more about the appearance of the doors. There was discussion of whether the baseboards were originally marbleized, but no evidence, even remnants of the glaze that usually accompanies marbleizing, was found prior to 1823. It was clear in the Entry Hall, however, that the door plinths were blue, which led Welsh to conclude that the Entry Hall baseboards were blue as well.

Written records showed that there had been wallpaper and borders above the chair rail, but most often they were not specific as to patterns. Often in restorations fragments of wallpaper are found around window frames or behind mantels when they are removed. Unfortunately no fragments were discovered in any places on the first floor. Photographs of the parlors taken at various times show that the mantels had been moved and replaced, and it was perhaps at these times that wallpaper evidence was destroyed in those areas. On the second floor and in the basement wallpaper pieces were found. We found much later papers, perhaps from the mid-1900s, on the second floor. In the basement, however, behind some lathing added at some unknown date, we found segments of paper dating perhaps to the first days of the dining room in the basement of the Governor's House.

History Confronts Modern Systems

The search for paint and wallpaper evidence was only the beginning of the decision making process about how the house would be restored. Once the basic research was completed, the decision had to be made as to which period or periods would be presented on the first floor and how modern systems would be integrated into the original building fabric. The Governor's House had changed in dramatic ways at several times during its existence, and the restoration needed to address these changes with a coherent, meaningful approach. This list of alterations, some additions as well as deletions, began before the residence was occupied, even for the first time. Indeed, before its initial construction in 1813 by Christopher Tompkins, alterations to the original Parris design had already been made, even those requiring additional funding by the legislature. The two side porches were added as the House was first built, but a groin vaulted entry, evidenced by supporting columns in Parris' notebook, may have been excluded for price considerations.[1] Changes of this sort to the exterior were addressed during the 1989 exterior renovation.

No doubt, the differences in lifestyles of the various families in residence demanded alterations not only in the way that rooms were used, but in their construction as well. Most governors of the 19th century greeted their guests in what is now known as the Old Governor's Office, while ladies who accompanied them waited across the broad Entry Hall in "the Reception Room," a matching front room now called the Ladies Parlor.

The rear of the house was intended to be more intimate and was closed off by a wall with a door for each of the back parlors. These two rooms, stretching across the entire back of the house, were originally used as a Drawing Room and Dining Room; on the Parris drawing they appear to be joined by a double wide door. In 1846 Governor William Smith moved the dining room from the first floor to the basement, and First Lady Etta Donnan Mann records in 1910 that "in the old days, as in so many of the early homes of Colonial Virginia, the dining-room was in the basement."[2] After this move, the double parlors were used as a large reception area.

In 1906 Duncan Lee's addition of a new Dining Room on the first floor, and his redesign of the back parlors into a large ballroom in the Colonial Revival style, introduced a second period into the décor; with some changes to the front door, the front parlors and hallway were still basically of the 1813 Alexander Parris design. *By 1998, the Lee "renovation" was almost a century old and historic in its own right, and thus all eras of the appearance of the house had to be considered in any renovation plans.*

The committee's decision to follow this complex historical development and create a coherent first floor was further complicated by the necessity of adding modern systems to the structure. Not only were HVAC, electrical and plumbing issues to be considered, but making the house handicap accessible for the first time was also a priority. Providing accessible entry and restroom facilities was a priority of the

Duncan Lee introduced Colonial Revival elements into his new, open Ballroom. Ceiling medallions replaced ceiling borders of the Parris rear parlors. Courtesy Library of Virginia

Fred Ecker of Tidewater Preservation, Inc., extensively examined the parquet floors to determine the best way to preserve them for current use and possible future methods of conservation. Courtesy DHR

The north side porch, damaged in the 1926 fire, was an addition made before the original construction of the house was completed. A new system of fire detection was added to prevent future disasters.

Courtesy Library of Virginia

44   Restoring the Virginia Governor's House

Gilmore administration and the focus of many of the planning sessions. Various solutions were examined. For example, one plan under consideration would have kept the elevator in its original location in the center of the house. This old elevator shaft exited onto the main floor in the arch of the pocket doors that led from the Ballroom to the Dining Room. The elevator was hardly large enough for one person and would have needed such expansion to be made accessible that the arched entry into the Dining Room would have had to be removed. This arch is a fundamental element of the Duncan Lee design of the first floor, echoing the original arch of Alexander Parris from the Entry Hall to the back parlors, and has been a dominant feature of the first floor for almost a century. Therefore we decided that removing the arch was not a tenable solution, and another plan had to be sought.

The parquet flooring that had been added in 1903 gave us issues of both conservation and style. Parquet, popular in Colonial Revival décor, had replaced the wide-board pine floors covered with Brussels carpet considered stylish during the earlier Federal period. The parquet was almost a century old, and there was no discussion of removing it or of totally covering it with wall-to-wall Brussels carpets. Tidewater Preservation Inc. studied this flooring extensively before the renovation was started. Over time, spiked heels and rough-bottomed shoes had taken their toll. Dents, scratches and stains abounded; in some places, small replacement boards had been nailed into place. Though some squeaking floor boards in historic buildings testify to a building's age and add to its charm, incessant squeaking throughout the first floor of the House was no longer considered charming. Saving the parquet and having it as an asset and not an annoyance was another facet of the renovation that became a priority as well as a main element in deciding how to approach the décor of the first floor.

Another critical element that we examined was making this historic house technology ready. The eve of the technical revolution was at hand and planning had to be made for the addition of systems that could grow as needed without severe changes to the building. There was no question that we had to make decisions for this new technology before the construction phase of the project.

Not all of our discoveries during the planning phase and initial demolitions were calamitous or cost related; many turned out to be "just interesting" and added to the lore of the house. As the demolition of the basement and second floor began, the historic quality of the building was confirmed by discoveries such as the wooden pegs we found in the basement ceiling still in place supporting the first floor. The chimney base for the hearth in the Old Governor's Office was found in the EPU office. It had an arched support that had a cabinet built into the arch. The probable location of the first central heating was found in the EPU office as well. It was an old furnace pit beneath vents that opened into the first floor Entry Hall. In the Director's office the whitewashed door jamb of a historic doorway was found on the east wall. We preserved this structure as shelving for the office.

Some of our discoveries were of a personal nature. Evidence of some of the earliest electrical wiring in the building was a note found in the ceiling area of the EPU Office which had the

A note signed by the team of electricians who wired the house in 1914 was found in the basement.   Courtesy DHR

Using Technology to Gather Historical Data

signatures of those men who installed the wiring. This note, dated October 1914, records the electricians who no doubt hastily decided to verify their presence at the House by each signing their name to a scrap piece of boxing left from the project and tacking it to the ceiling before it was plastered.

As walls were removed in the second floor and basement, many remnants of wallpapers were found. Some were modern and had been chosen by more recent residents. Others were older, dating to perhaps the later 19th century, with pink roses apparently being favored in many administrations. One of the most intriguing, and perhaps the oldest, wall covering from the early 19th century era of the house was found in the basement area behind some lathing where the Dining Room of "Extra Billy" Smith may have been. We had hoped that some of the original papers like this one would be found, and we chose to have this antique pattern with its Greek key border and pattern reproduced and placed in the Lafayette Bedroom.

The demolition of the second floor gave an unexpected glimpse of one of the most riveting events in the history of the Governor's House. Along the walls and ceiling of the room over the north side of the Ballroom were smoked-stained timbers and wall-coverings, surely evidence of the January 1926 fire which started in the north Ballroom. Repair to the fire damage had been done rapidly so that Governor Byrd and his family could move in as soon as possible after his inauguration, and it was perhaps due to that time pressure that some of the damage was left and only covered over.

Historic restoration is a painstaking process that requires diligence, patience and, most especially, commitment. Since sources of information are many and often disparate, it takes total dedication to the project to search all of the evidence and use it to best advantage. However, another large part of preservation is restraint. Not finding an answer during research does not create a *tabula rasa* for new work. Once historic building material is removed, it is gone forever; thus changes that remove building fabric must be done judiciously. The first rule is to do no harm, so that if future research turns up new evidence or new methods of preservation are created, they can be incorporated at a later time. Our research efforts encountered several issues of this very nature, such as the restoration of the front parlor mantels and the first floor parquet floors. We used the best methods available at the time to stop the deterioration of these features and save them for some possible future process. As more families come and go, there will be more work done on the Governor's House that will continue to save its historic features and add to the life of the building.

CHAPTER 6

The Hallway, a Janus

Our selection of a stylistic period for the front parlors of the Governor's House was not difficult because the rooms had changed very little since Alexander Parris originally designed them, and it was clear that these rooms should reflect the Federal period of their origin. However, treatment of the Entry Hall was more challenging because of the many major changes that had been made in its design over the years. Parquet floors had been installed throughout the first floor in 1903, using this later style element from the front of the house to the rear. These floors, combined with the sweeping changes made by Duncan Lee in 1906, significantly altered the 1813 appearance of the first floor as one enters the house.

In the original Parris design, the first floor of the House contained two basic areas: the public front parlors and two rear rooms intended for private gatherings. The rear rooms were separated by a partition from the front of the house. When Andrew Jackson Montague became Governor in 1902, little work had been done to the interior of the House for some years. Photographs taken during the administration of Governor Charles O'Ferrall (January 1, 1894, through January 1,

A wire strung from the chandelier gave electricity to the lamp on Governor O'Ferrell's desk.
Courtesy Library of Virginia

1898) show a mass of furniture crammed into the Governor's Office and electric wires strung from the chandelier to a lamp on the governor's desk. Immediately upon moving into the House, Governor Montague and his wife, Betsie, turned their attention to updating what was by now being called the Executive Mansion—painting, acquiring new furniture, and, most significantly, installing parquet floors were the tasks that the Montagues undertook. A photograph of daughter Gay Montague's George Washington's birthday party in 1903 shows that the parquet floors were already in place by February 1903, and the photographs of the parlors taken prior to the visit of Theodore Roosevelt in 1905 show these floors covered with Oriental carpets.[1] The rooms contained an eclectic assortment of furniture with both Victorian pieces and some newly acquired Colonial pieces favored by the Montagues. Painted walls reflected the style of the day with deep reds in the rear parlors and other dark colors in the front rooms as well.

Though refurbished by the Montagues, the Governor's House still suffered from structural disrepair and a lack of space. After his inauguration in 1906, Governor Claude A. Swanson obtained General Assembly funding for Duncan Lee to make major design changes to the first floor. Lee's ideas incorporated the latest rage in decorating in the country, Colonial Revival. After its grand introduction at the US Centennial

The newly opened Ballroom of Duncan Lee had a mixture of furnishings including a Victrola to provide music. Governor Byrd is reported to have sold the state limousine in order to buy a grand piano.   Courtesy Library of Virginia

Exposition in 1876, Colonial Revival elements remained popular in American tastes until the mid–1950s, and some elements are still popular today. Casting aside the ornate embellishments characteristic of the Victorian age, Colonial Revival returned to simpler forms. Lee was masterful at including the essentials of this new hybrid of traditional styles–central hallways, colonnades, a new front door with sidelights and transom. He skillfully added all of these elements to the Classical elements already put in place by Alexander Parris and created rooms that were elegant and unified in their appearance.

One of Lee's main changes was to design a large Dining Room which would be housed in a completely new addition on the rear of the house. The Governor's House had always lacked adequate space for receptions and dinners, and a new focus on entertaining increased this need. Etta Donnan Mann, wife of Governor William Hodges Mann, recorded in her diary in February 1910 that "In the old days, as in so many of the early homes of Colonial Virginia, the dining-room was in the basement."[2] She wrote this while commenting on her good fortune to be able to move into a newly renovated Governor's House that included the beautiful Duncan Lee Dining Room on the first floor. She and her husband would actually be the first to benefit from this room since it was added during the term of their predecessors, the Swansons, and changes of this magnitude certainly must have been disruptive to their time in the residence.

Perhaps the most dramatic change that Lee made was to eliminate the rear, intimate spaces and create a first floor that was grand and open throughout. He removed the wall separating the public and private areas and unified this vast new space with a central hall that stretched from the front door to the east wall of the newly added Dining Room. On this wall in the Dining Room, which opposes the front door, he placed a mantled fireplace as the focal element for the new hall. This door to fireplace vista bisects the large space that has come to be known as the Ballroom which Mrs. Mann referred to as "a reception hall that stretched the full width of the house."[3]

The new central hallway bisects the Ballroom with two rows of columns. Lee used the columns to keep the sense of the original two back parlors, but at the same time leave a completely open expanse. It is this vast sense of space that impresses everyone entering the front door of the Governor's House, especially after approaching the exterior, which is less than formidable in appearance. While it is the front-to-back view from the hall that usually has the greatest impact on visitors, Mrs. Mann commented on the reverse view that is not often noticed. Perhaps standing in the Dining Room for one of her first official functions, she wrote that from the Dining Room, there "stretches a wonderful vista, showing the Washington monument in the distance."[4] These views, from both directions, must be precisely the impression that Duncan Lee wished to make on anyone entering or being entertained in the Governor's House.

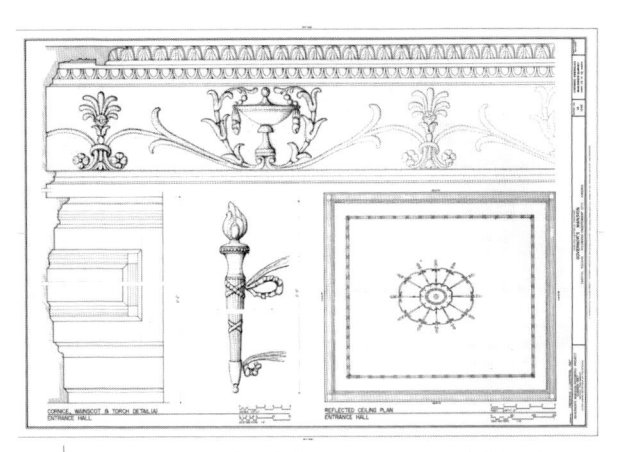

A 1987 National Park Service project recorded the plaster and cornice work of the historic rooms. The elements of the entrance hall are shown in this drawing.
Courtesy Library of Virginia

Though Lee chose to change the Governor's House from a closed, small-roomed house to one

The Hallway, a *Janus* 49

Today an elaborate central medallion of ribbon-joined torches surrounds the entrance hall chandelier.   Courtesy DHR

that was grand and open, he did not cast aside all of the Parris design elements from the front hall. When he removed the partition into the back of the house, Lee kept the Classical beaded arch that Parris had used to decorate the Entry Hall as well as the Classical frieze. Lee not only kept the arch, but he copied it with a series of arches as entries to the Ballroom and Dining Room. By using this repetition of such a dominating architectural feature, he unified the new rooms that he had created and prevented them from being just cavernous spaces.

It was probably during the Lee renovation that changes were made to the ceiling decorations. Photographs taken prior to Lee's work show that there were ornamental plaster borders on all of the first floor ceilings. The original hall ceiling border was the most elaborate, with a torch in a laurel garland at each corner; the photographs do not show if there is anything at the base of the hall chandelier. In addition to the ceiling decorations, the Entry Hall had a cornice decorated with torches, urns, and foliage. The rear parlor ceilings had borders similar to the front parlors.

After 1906 only the front parlor borders remained as they had been. In the Entry Hall the torches were removed from the corners of the ceiling border and an elaborate central medallion with torches and garlands reminiscent of those originally in the corners was added. In the new Ballroom the borders were removed completely and medallions were added to the base of the chandeliers. Paint research by Frank Welsh supports the time of these changes, with no evidence earlier than the 1920s seen on the ceilings.[5] The repair of damage from the fire in 1926 could account for the lack of evidence earlier than the 1920s, but the pictures taken after the Lee additions are clear about the changes made to the ceilings.

During the 1998 renovation the impact that Duncan Lee had left on the Governor's House could not be overlooked. His dramatic alterations had resulted in a mixture of periods on the first floor, and it was impossible to ignore either Lee's sweeping changes or the surviving Parris embellishments, which were still significant. This is particularly true in the hall, which was no longer a one-room entry but now swept from front the door to the rear of the house. This hall had to retain the continued influence of both architects and allow the visitor to move easily between the two–the remaining front Federal parlors or the Colonial Revival Ballroom and Dining Room.

John Paul Hanbury referred to the Entry Hall as the *"Janus,"* a space that, like the Roman god Janus, looked to the future and the past. Relying on the extant Parris form of the front spaces and Duncan Lee's obvious effort to create a seamless segue from the Entry Hall to the Dining Room, the 1998 renovation used special treatment for the hallway designed to represent both the 1813 era and the later Colonial Revival period; neither could be exclusive in this entry space.

Once we decided to treat the hall as a *Janus*, the principle question was how to accomplish this goal. The paint research done by Frank Welsh provided the unifying element needed to proceed. In fact, the paint findings became the fundamental basis for making most choices of décor on the first floor. Welsh's paint analysis produced something of a surprise when it reported that in the hall "the plaster walls retain substantial evidence to indicate that they were painted with a medium gray, lead-based paint."[6] The final

John Paul Hanbury kept the Citizens Advisory Committee informed as discoveries were made in paint research and decisions were made about using that information.   Courtesy DHR

decision to rely on these findings was not without question.

I'll never forget the day that I received the results of the paint analysis done to determine the original colors of the house: 'Gray wainscoting and mantels and brown baseboards and tops of chair rails.' How exciting (translated–drab!), I thought. Though drab sounding, this revelation turned out to be probably the most significant information discovered in the planning phase of the renovation, and it became the basis for the most significant decisions we made in the entire project.

The initial choice of color was critical to the project in many ways and is an excellent example of how design and schedule were dependent on each other for the success of the restoration. First, the selection of colors of these prominent features would drive the choice of colors and fabrics for the entire first floor, a decision sure to be noticed. Gray and brown would create an entirely new color scheme and would differ drastically from the pastel tones that had greeted visitors before. For many years the Entry Hall had been painted a pale yellow, joining the white plaster frieze and making the frieze almost disappear into the ceiling. Moving away from this popular image of the hall would be dramatic. Second, the hall was no longer a separate room as it had been in the original Parris design, and its inextricable connection

The yellow paint used in the entrance hall did not display the white cornices and arches to their best advantage.   Courtesy DHR

The Hallway, a *Janus* 51

to the Ballroom and Dining Room had to be taken into consideration in color selections. Maintaining Lee's vision of unity on the first floor had to be considered in the choice of colors. Finally, an early decision on color choice was necessary because of the impact it would have on the production schedule of furnishings for the first floor rooms. The carpets and many of the fabrics were to be hand loomed, and the extensive time involved in producing these fabrics meant that they had to be ordered while the construction was ongoing.[7] Early ordering would ensure that the upholstery and drapery fabrics would be completed by the time the structural work was finished. All of this meant that the decision about the basic color of the front parlors and hall had to be among the first made in the project.

Because gray would be so different from the yellow everyone was used to, part of the wall was painted to see what it would look like. The beautiful moldings and frieze came to life and the decision was made to use gray. Courtesy DHR

The doors had enough paint evidence to show they had been faux finished mahogany, popular in 1813. Courtesy DHR

Despite the urgency of John Paul Hanbury's greeting to me each time he came to the Governor's House "Have you decided yet?", I took some time before making a final decision. To help me decide whether to make this drastic change in color, I asked to see what gray would look like, so one of the walls in the Ladies' Parlor was painted in the proposed shade of gray. But the existing pink walls of that room next to the gray made it extremely difficult to tell how anything would appear. Seeing some choices of wallpaper and fabrics that would blend with the gray helped.

Most importantly, the opportunity that I had in January 1999 to visit the Stourvale Rug Mill in Kidderminster, England, gave me uniquely helpful insights. While at the mill I examined original carpet patterns from the early 19th century. Handwritten on the backs of these antique patterns were the colors suggested for their production–drab, light drab, and dark drab. In the early 19th century drab was the term used for grays, taupes and beiges and lacked the pejorative meaning that it has today. In fact, the frequency with which it appeared on these patterns indicates that it was in fact a very popular family of colors. Nonetheless, it remained a difficult choice to make between these "drab" colors and the pale yellow interior and white woodwork that was on the walls.

Our decision finally was sealed when one last trial was made–painting one of the Entry Hall walls gray where Welsh's research had shown gray as the original color. Immediately the white plaster sprung to life next to the gray background, making it the significant feature it was intended to be. No lon-

52 Restoring the Virginia Governor's House

ger did the plaster frieze disappear into the ceiling. The torches, draped urns, and trailing foliage were instantly recognizable and provided the classical impression they were meant to inspire. The hall now resembled an elegant piece of Wedgwood china. Our choice was made—the research had decided this matter and gray it would be!

In addition to wall coloration, Welsh's research also gave information about the coloring on the plinth blocks of the hall doorways to the side rooms and some of the trim in the hall. The plinth blocks showed a very dark blue oil paint and led to the conclusion that the vertical faces of the baseboards were similarly treated. Though extensive paint removal at various times had destroyed evidence on the chair rails in the hall, Welsh concluded that they were probably treated with the same dark brown that had been found in the side parlors. The two original doors had enough paint evidence to indicate that they had been grained to imitate a reddish brown mahogany, a very popular process in Richmond homes in 1813.

Not only did we use these findings to determine how the hall would be treated, but we also relied on Welsh's findings in the hall to decide how the hall and the Ballroom and Dining Room would be unified in accordance with the plan of Duncan Lee; we incorporated the hall's historic wall, plaster, and baseboard colors throughout to maintain this relationship. The white accent of the hall ceiling plaster and friezes, brought to life by the return to gray walls, continues into the Ballroom with its use on the Corinthian columns marking the original parlors. These columns illustrate the real Colonial Revival impact of the Ball-

The finished hall was the Janus Hanbury desired. Its gray walls accented the Parris arches and friezes while the loose-laid Brussels carpet introduced the new style of the Ballroom. Courtesy Library of Virginia

room since columns and white trim are hallmarks of this style. Further relying on the paint research that showed that by 1823 marbleizing was used in the Governor's House, we marbleized the column bases to tie the blue baseboards of the hall to the column bases. This blue was furthered transferred to the Ballroom through the use of a predominantly blue document wallpaper border. Gray walls completed the seamless segue into the rear rooms and created the same look that Lee made when he had placed gray, Louis XVI wallpaper into the newly opened Ballroom.[8] Thus Duncan Lee's goal of opening the house by removing the separating partition is maintained by the use of these continuous elements of original color.

Historically documented rug patterns were loomed in specially chosen colors for the entrance hall and front parlor carpets.
Courtesy DHR

Continuing the approach of using the hallway as a *Janus* led to the decisions made in treating the hall floors. Because the gray of the original 1813 décor was to be used on the walls, and because the hall joined the two 1813 period parlors, it seemed appropriate to use Brussels carpeting of that same period on the floors. Since the parquet throughout the first floor was almost a century old, however, it seemed inappropriate to lay the carpet wall-to-wall as would have been customary in the Federal period. After much consideration we chose a dark red wool Brussels carpet with black and gray stars and wreaths for the hall. It is a design of the Federal period from an 1806 point paper, and its border repeats the elaborate woodwork of the Parris hallway and hints at the 1813 décor of the flanking parlors. But instead of laying this carpet wall-to-wall, we had it bound and loose-laid like an Oriental to allow the parquet to be seen and to transition smoothly between the Federal Brussels carpets of the hall and the Oriental carpets appropriately placed in the Colonial Revival Ballroom.

A slight modification of the Brussels carpet had to be made in order to use the carpet in the staircases that are off of the main hall. At the back of the main hall is a narrow hallway that runs across the house to the side porch exits. There is also a staircase on each side of the hall that goes up to the second floor living area. However, the staircases are not the same width, a detail that created a problem in continuing the hall carpeting up the staircases. The repeat of the carpet pattern with its wreaths and stars was greater than the width of the narrower of the two staircases and could not be used in that space. To accommodate this difference, only the stars from the field of the main rug were used in the stair carpeting. This accomplished both the need to keep the hall and staircase carpets the same, and it also helped disguise the difference in the stair widths.

To complete the *Janus*, we selected furnishings that transition into both parlors and the Ballroom. The 1815 crystal and ormolu English Regency chandelier remained in the hallway and is one of the oldest fixtures in the House. It pairs with the Regency chandelier in the Dining Room, and the two chandeliers' Federal style reflects the decorative details present in the earliest days of the Governor's House.

We hung a pair of 1810 gilt cavetto framed convex mirrors on opposite walls, flanking the doorway. One of the mirrors was placed above a circa 1812, eagle-based, marble topped pier table attributed to Duncan Phyfe. The table, a gift of Mr. and Mrs. Nick Matthews of Yorktown, is ebonized and has gilt paw feet. The other mirror was above a mahogany Sheraton "chair back" settee, a late 18th century piece attributed to Henry Connelly of Philadelphia. It has a rare "four chair" back, and we had a seat cushion made with a gold on cream Classical Wreath fabric by Scalamandre.

A 1795 signed Ettingham Embree New York case clock, gift of Mr. and Mrs. Harwood Cochrane of Rockville, keeps perfect time and chimes on the hour. Its mahogany case with an eagle inlay majestically flanked the door into the Old Governor's Office and faced a portrait of the great Virginian, Thomas Jefferson, on loan from Washington and Lee University. Portraits of other Colonial Virginians, James Monroe and George Washington, on loan from Kenmore, flanked the arched doorway that leads into the grand Ballroom.

With the hall treated as a *Janus*, guests to the Governor's House are greeted with elements of style of the two architects who have had the most impact on its appearance. The Federal style of Alexander Parris even now forms the basis of the first floor, still dramatically visible in the beaded arches or subtly whispered in the remaining vestiges of the back parlors. The colors chosen and the type of rug secure Parris' touch in the hall. Likewise, Lee's impact on the house is evident even before entering. A new transom and windows flanking the door are hints of the changes waiting inside. Lee's move to open the house created a grand hall that draws one into the interior by his repetition of the original Parris arch throughout the downstairs. Our use of color and furnishings combined the vision of both architects and created a harmonious linchpin for the remaining historic rooms.

Facing west in the center of the Ballroom, one has this view of the Entry Hall which is flanked by the 1813 parlors. Because this room contains elements from both the Parris and Lee eras, the restored room was designed to be a segue from the 1813 parlors to the 1906 Ballroom and Dining Room.

Courtesy Library of Virginia

CHAPTER 7

The 1813 Rooms

Flanking the Entry Hall are the two rooms that have remained the most true to their original Alexander Parris design. On the northwest corner, the Old Governor's Office was originally used by governors as a working office or library. As late as 1905 a photograph shows that the governor still continued to conduct much public business in this room. Located on the southeast corner, is the Ladies' Parlor where women and families who had accompanied their husbands to see the Governor's House would be entertained. In form, these rooms were identical. Each had two windows on the west façade and one on the end. Each room also had a pair of doors on the east wall that exited into a narrow hallway that ran between the parlors on the front of the house and the more private rooms in the back. The symmetry of these rooms was characteristic of houses of the Federal period and was an important element to keep.

Of the two parlors, the structural design of the Old Governor's Office had been altered the most over the years. The two doors exiting the room on the east wall had been removed, and the room could be entered only from the main hall. While both of these east wall doors survived in the Ladies' Parlor, only one of the doors was actually used to enter and exit, with the other permanently locked. The area behind the locked door of the Ladies' Parlor and one of the lost doorways in the Governor's office had been used to build in cabinets in the side hall to display the silver service from the Battleship USS Virginia. These cabinets were constructed at the request of First Lady Josephine Almond in the late 1950s after she had managed to secure the return of the silver from the Navy to the Commonwealth. The second door in the Governor's Office had been closed in order to construct a display case for the Steuben glass bowl that the

In the 1890s Governor O'Ferrell's office was filled with furniture. A screen covered the dark, heavy fireplace. It was to this old style that Governor and Mrs. Montague began to introduce new style elements of Colonial Revival, seen in the 1905 photos in Chapter 1.

Courtesy Library of Virginia

A doorway into the Old Governor's Office from a side hall formed a cabinet for storing the Battleship Silver. Courtesy DHR

President of Corning Glass presented to Governor Albertis Harrison and the citizens of Virginia when a new Corning plant was opened in Danville in 1962. There was also a small half-bath at the end of the northside hall, the only restroom on the first floor. Because we wished to be true to the 1813 design of Parris and we believed that the movement of visitors through the house would be more fluid, we decided to return the doors to the Governor's Office and reopen the second door in the Ladies' Parlor. This necessitated the removal of the tiny restroom as well as the removal of the storage cases for the Battleship silver and Steuben glass.

The removal of the restroom was not a problem since the decision had been made to put an accessible restroom elsewhere on the first floor and the Steuben bowl would have a new display case in this same area. Finding an alternative way of displaying the silver could be accommodated as well. The silver display cases were problematic in any case. Though they provided adequate space, seeing the individual pieces was difficult. Lighting was insufficient, and larger pieces such as the punch bowl had to be

58 Restoring the Virginia Governor's House

displayed on the bottom shelf. The punch bowl has pictures of seven of the eight Virginia presidents, and if positioned on the bottom shelf, just those on the front of the bowl were visible and then only by kneeling on the floor to get to their level! In traveling to other Executive residences which had acquired their state's battleship silver, I noticed that their collections were proudly displayed in the open. Noting as well that the Battleship Virginia silver was commissioned in 1906, the same year that the Dining Room was added, it seemed appropriate to use the silver in the Dining Room and the punch bowl with Virginia's presidents in the center of the Ballroom where visitors could see it from all sides. Once we settled on this, the road was clear to restore the doors into the Governor's Office.

Re-adding the doors to the Old Governor's Office would require cutting the walls and making new doorframes–or that is what we thought. But as the first cuts were made in the wall, we discovered that the doors were still in place and just plastered over. The door jambs had served as the core structure of the display cases and only some minor adjustments had to be made to the framework. As in many restoration projects, our research was enhanced by the foresight of those who had made earlier changes and had chosen not to destroy the historic elements of the building.

Structure was not the only common element shared by the two parlors. The paint research by Frank Welsh showed that the "two side parlors were treated identically when first painted."[1] The baseboards, plinth blocks, cap moldings of the chair rails, and shelves of the two mantelpieces were painted a dark brown. The remaining trim and mantelpieces were painted the same light gray that was in the front hallway. Surface evidence indicated that wallpaper had covered the walls above the wainscoting, though in this testing we found no original fragments.

A door from the Old Governor's Office into an adjoining hall had been walled over to form a small restroom on the other side. Both doors from the office were restored in 1999.
Courtesy DHR

Just as the paint research was followed in returning to the original gray as the basic color in the hall and throughout the first floor, the same research was used to make decisions for the parlors. Based on these results the wainscoting and mantels in both rooms were painted gray with brown baseboards and chair rails. The only deviation was to paint the mantels entirely gray and not make their tops brown. The doors were faux finished to look like mahogany and fitted with brass box locks, again following the research results.

Though attempts were made to find original wallpaper in the front parlors, Mr. Welsh discovered no fragments. He recommended that more testing be done at some future time when larger pieces of the existing canvas wall covering could be removed in more strategic locations. Because of the similarity in the other results for the two rooms, we chose the same basic wallpaper to cover above the wainscoting. Barbara Page searched for the perfect paper in existing document wallpaper patterns and patterns known to have been used in a certain historic period. "Seedwell," a pattern by Bailey and Griffin, is a gray paper with a darker gray Greek anthemion pattern. The anthemion, a stylized honeysuckle pattern popular in the early

LEFT: *Pink dominated the Ladies' Parlor though the restored mantel began to introduce the new gray into the room.*
RIGHT: *Workmen begin to carefully remove the mantel in the Old Governor's Office to take it off site for refurbishment.* Courtesy DHR

19th century, became an element that tied all the rooms together because of its repeated use in many of the textiles throughout the house.

To add to this basic plan for both parlors, we chose an 1810 document rug pattern for use in both rooms. This design was hand loomed by Woodward and Grosvenor at the Stourvale Mill in Kidderminster, England. The specific pattern chosen had as one of its dominant features a "spider web" pattern that was similar to the web of the plaster in the ceilings of both parlors.

Two other similar features of the parlors were the carved wood and plaster mantelpieces, each serving as the primary focus in its own room. These mantels became special preservation projects in their own right. Damaged over time by layers and layers of paint and by "aggressive" attempts to remove all of these layers, the plaster composite figures on these mantels were almost unrecognizable. A team of conservators composed of Catherine S. Myers of Myers Conservation, Washington, DC, and Fred Ecker and Greg Cowen of Tidewater Preservation Inc. in Fredericksburg, oversaw the removal and study of these mantels. In her interim report on August 12, 1999 to John Paul Hanbury, Myers said:

> . . . discussions have centered on how to achieve aesthetic unity without falsifying the mantels' authenticity and at once retaining the evidence of changes and alterations. The approach developed for handling these losses has been guided by principles for practice as established by the international conservations charters and the American Institute for Conservation of Historic and Artistic Works.[2]

This was exactly the adherence to accepted restoration standards that we were trying to achieve on the project; therefore, we followed the recommendations of this team carefully.

Though some early photographs show the front parlors with different mantelpieces in place, after their removal for conservation we decided that these were probably the original mantels to these rooms because of the way they were hung on the fireplace bricks. The paint research done by Frank Welsh confirmed this belief. At some time when the fashion was to have marble-lined mantels, these painted mantels were moved to the upstairs bedrooms. In 1903 when then Governor Montague made changes to the first floor, he is said to have removed the Victorian-era marble mantels from the front parlors, broken them up, and lined the driveway with the pieces. We found marble pieces in the parking area outside the Carriage House when the West Gate was excavated. Montague supposedly returned the original mantels from the upstairs bedrooms to their rightful places in the front parlors. Although this story is often told, it is contradicted by photographs. The 1905 picture of the Old Governor's Office at the time of Teddy Roosevelt's visit shows the marble mantel still in place. The original mantels were probably returned during Governor Swanson's major work on the Mansion in 1906, though there is also evidence that Governor Elbert Lee Trinkle ordered new mantels in the Ballroom in the 1920s and was disappointed when he realized they were plaster and not carved wood.

Once the mantels were at the conservation studio and the layers of paint removed, we found that much of the mantel material was gone. The figures on the mantel were formed with a composite of sawdust, hide glue and sometimes plaster, and earlier paint removal using heat had melted these figures. Often there was not enough left to know what had been there and how it should be restored. Because of this loss, and on the recommendation of the conservators, we decided not to restore lost and damaged areas of the mantels in case some later research or the discovery of photographs could determine what should correctly be restored. One of the primary goals of the project was to make restorations when enough evidence was found to support those restorations, such as the use of the original paint colors found after research. What we avoided was doing more harm to objects by guessing or using personal preference to make "restorations" when there was no supporting data. The mantels fell into this "do no harm" category.

Despite the loss of so much of the original work, there was much to be learned about both of the mantels. The mantel in the Governor's office has basic Masonic and military themes. Considering the looming 1812 British forces in America when the house was under construction, it is not surprising that cannonballs and crossed flags appear here. These elements were cleaned and made much more recognizable. However, the "dolphin" pillars hold up mystery objects that were not replaced because they could not be identified. Mysteries about the mantel in the Ladies' Parlor were laid to rest though. The center of the mantel in the Ladies' Parlor depicts a woman in a chariot with a baby in her lap; before the layers of paint were removed, Secretary of Administration Bryan Slater joked that the blob in the lady's lap had to be a basketball!

The final shared decisions for the two parlors involved the new HVAC (heating, ventilation, and air conditioning) and fire suppression systems. Efforts were made to hide the addition of these modern systems in these rooms and preserve as much of the original fabric of the building as possible. Adding and hiding these systems without completely gouging the walls presented numerous challenges. To add wiring, fire suppression

A close-up view of the dolphin detail on the mantel in the Old Governor's Office shows the damage that had been done in the past using heat to remove paint.
Courtesy DHR

access, and access for the new HVAC system, cuts in the wall had to be made as small as possible. I spent one of the hottest days of 1998 going from the crawl space under Mount Vernon to the top of its cupola to learn how its staff had decided to install the historic building's new HVAC system and how difficult it was to determine how much (or little) to cut away. I was able to see the brick foundation underlying the main house when I was taken to see vent work being installed. Whenever possible, the cuts they made to take the vents through the house were made in such out-of-the-way areas as closet interiors or other places not in ready view. But always as little as possible of the building's historic fabric was destroyed. Again, the willingness of experts like Mount Vernon Executive Director James C. Rees, IV to share their knowledge made our decisions much easier and led to the success of the end result at the Governor's House.[3]

In order to add new fire sprinklers and smoke detectors as inconspicuously as possible, we placed them in the wallpaper borders at the base of the ceiling. The vents for the HVAC system were handmade and discreetly put on the top of the baseboards below the windows; each section of the baseboard had to be separately hand cut to accommodate the addition of the HVAC vents. The vents were painted to match the baseboards which further disguised them. Visitors to the House are always amazed at how difficult it is to detect these systems and impressed with the lengths that we took to hide these modern conveniences.

The Old Governor's Office

While the major features of the walls, carpets, and mantel colors were identical in the two parlors, two unique, specially appointed rooms emerged. The Old Governor's Office was returned to a dignified, business-like appearance—a suitable space where a governor could work or meet constituents. It had a sense of strength and dignity reflected in its furnishings.

A handsome, masculine appearance of the Old Governor's Office was achieved despite its shared basic wallpaper and carpet with the Ladies' Parlor. The wallpaper border at the ceiling is a pattern that Scalamandre revived from their archives just for the Governor's House renovation. When I visited the Scalamandre mill in New York in June 1999 and looked through some of their document wallpaper patterns, I particularly liked a gray, black and gold pattern dominated by Greek lyres. The pattern was no longer being produced, but Scalamandre's President, Bob Bitter agreed to consider the possibility of reviving it. To my surprise and honor, Scalamandre not only placed the pattern back into production, but they also renamed the pattern "Roxane's Lyre."

The draperies of the Governor's Office are Versailles red wool St. James damask appropriate to 1813. They are lined with a gold silk fabric that was recycled from the draperies that used to hang in the Ballroom. Those draperies were no longer useful for the Ballroom, but were far too good in quality to discard. Racks of old draperies were already in storage, having been replaced by earlier administrations, and to add to this number seemed unnecessary.

Although the renovation necessitated buying new materials, we sought to conserve the many things of value present in the house. Ruth Hubbard, our seamstress from the Colonial Williamsburg Drapery Studio, had determined there was just enough of the fabric from these old draperies to use as linings for the draperies in both the Governor's Office and the Ladies' Parlor; thus, we avoided waste and did not have to buy any new lining material.

We placed the portrait of James Barbour, the first governor to reside here, over an 1820s mahogany bow front chest. Scalamandre renamed the wallpaper border used here "Roxane's Lyre."
Courtesy Library of Virginia

    The tassels on the new draperies were handmade, wooden mold tassels by Scalamandre. At the mill, groups of women hand-wrapped dark red silk, which matches the fabric of the drapes, around hand-carved wooden molds to make the tassels. Ruth Hubbard and her team then hand-sewed each tassel with gold and black silk onto red, gold, and black tape along the drapery borders.

    To furnish the Old Governor's Office we included numerous period antiques which have been given to the Governor's House by many benefactors. Many were given through the Citizens Advisory Committee over the years. We chose to coordinate these furnishings with the red and black of the draperies. An early 1800s Chippendale wing chair, gift of the Honorable and Mrs. Elmon Gray, was upholstered in black leather and flanks the hearth next to a dark red and black horsehair bench. Senator Gray represented the old 16th Senatorial district, following in the footsteps of his father, Peck Gray. Like his father, he ran the Gray Lumber Company sawmill in Waverly, about 25 miles south of Petersburg.

    A walnut Queen Anne English slip seat corner chair dated to 1750 was upholstered in black leather and accompanied a mahogany Chippendale block-front writing desk. The desk, circa 1780, has three interior shells and ball and claw feet. These two pieces had been gifts to the house of Mrs. Charles Beatty Moore.

The 1813 Rooms   63

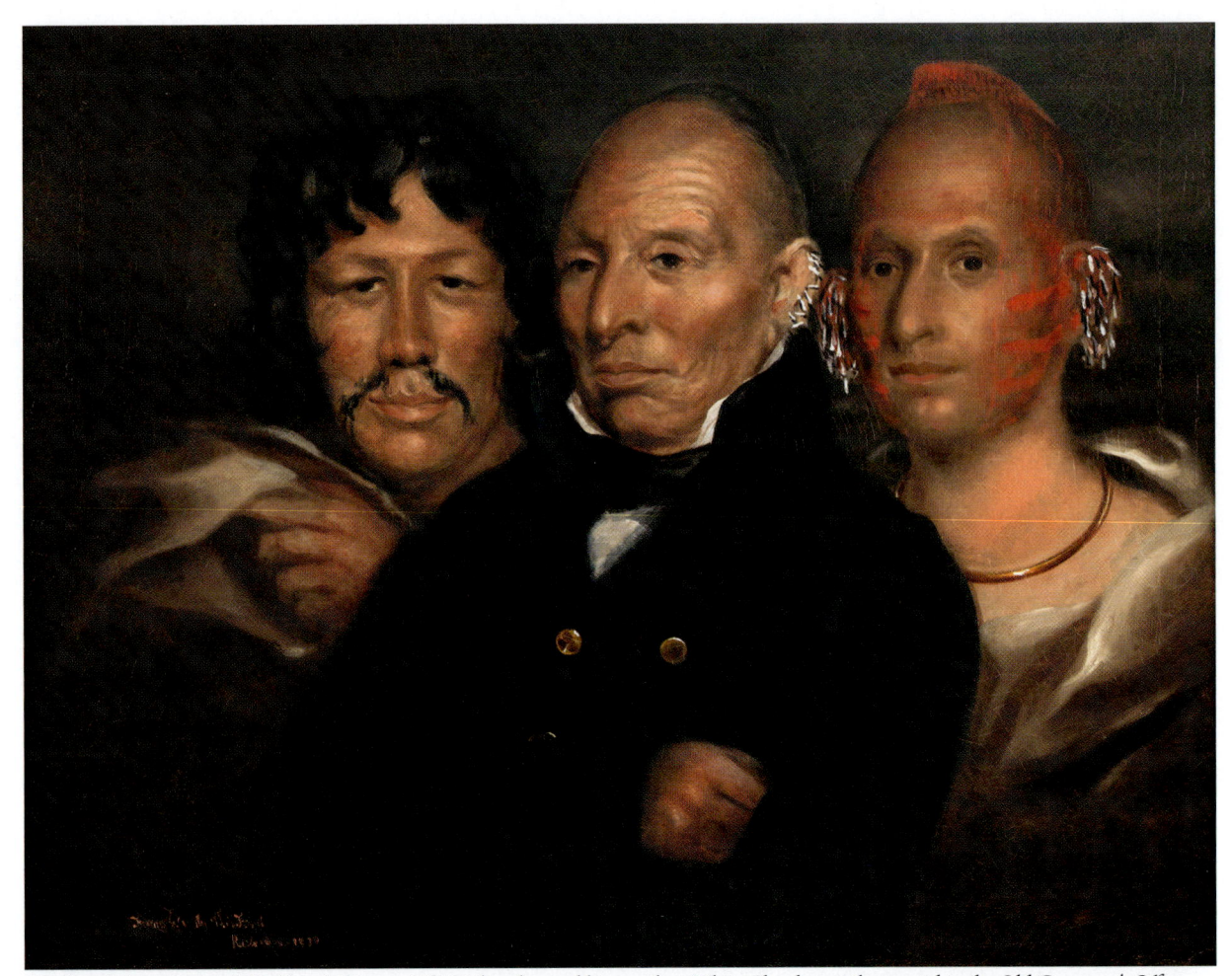

We placed the portrait of Blackhawk, his son, White Thunder, and his prophet, White Cloud, over the mantel in the Old Governor's Office. Visitors were fascinated by the story of Blackhawk's role in the War of 1812, contemporaneous with the construction of the Governor's House. The image belies their later position as captives to President Andrew Jackson.　　　　　Courtesy Library of Virginia

Mrs. Moore was Gay Montague, the daughter of Governor Andrew Jackson Montague, and she lived in the house from 1902 to 1906. Though these pieces were not used in the house during Montague's administration, Mrs. Moore's life in the house makes these pieces particularly special.

Next to the desk we placed an English, mahogany terrestrial globe by Cary, a gift of The Daughters of the American Revolution. These globes were made after Captain Cook's voyages in 1779 to update world maps and would have been of interest to gentlemen who may have called on the governor.

The mahogany bow front chest that we used in the Old Governor's Office has a banded and reeded top. It dates to the 1820s and was a bequest of Mrs. Nancy Chapman Wallower of Washington, D.C., formerly of Smithfield, Virginia. Beneath the north window was a walnut round tilt top lamp table with snake legs, reputed to be from the home of Patrick Henry, the Commonwealth's first governor. This table was a gift of Mrs. H.C.L. Miller of Richmond. A mahogany serpentine double top drop leaf card table sits along the wall at the side door into the hallway.

Guided skillfully by Tracy Kamerer, the Curator of the state's art collection, we chose the paintings for the Old Governor's Office to reflect the history of the governorship as well as of Virginia. The portrait of

James Barbour, the first governor to occupy the Governor's House and use the Old Governor's Office, was hung over the bow front chest on the wall opposite the front hall door. The portrait was moved from the Entry Hall to the focal point of this room so that it is the first thing one sees upon entering the room. Over the mantel we chose to place the oil-on-canvas portrait of the Indian Chief Blackhawk, his son, Whirling Thunder, and his prophet, White Cloud, painted by James Westhall Ford in 1833. This portrait is a favorite of visitors who are always mesmerized by the story of Blackhawk and his family. Blackhawk, born in 1767 was a supporter of the British in the War of 1812 and became distressed over the loss of Indian lands as settlers began to move westward. He led a rebellion of braves in The Black Hawk War when some of the settlers attacked a group of Indians traveling under a flag of truce. The painting shows Black Hawk as a hostage, forced by President Andrew Jackson to wear western attire as a symbol of submission. Few who see the painting find Black Hawk a deferential figure. A framed land grant signed by Patrick Henry in January 1784 was a gift of Mrs. Page B. Clagett of Washington, DC, and hung over the block-front desk.

All of these furnishings gave the Old Governor's Office the stature worthy of the office of the Governor of the Commonwealth. Today it can again accommodate the same type of business meetings for which it was originally designed, but also comfortably welcome guests during the many receptions held there.

The Ladies' Parlor

In contrast to the strong, masculine appointments of the Old Governor's Office, we gave the Ladies' Parlor a bright, feminine touch for the front of the house. The multi-colored, floral wallpaper border, borrowed from the late 18th century Mecklenburg County, Virginia estate of Prestwould, brought instant life to this room. The gold, blue, and light red border invited the use of those colors throughout the room. Gold silk swags and trims, with fabric rescued from the Ballroom, accented the dominating raspberry Watteau silk taffeta draperies. The gold brilliantly transferred to the 1800 Sheraton-style single cushion mahogany sofa in the antique gold silk fabric called "L'Adeille et le Guirland" ("The Bee and the Garland.") The lolling chairs picked up the light red of the border in their striped, shirred silk fabric. A pair of mahogany shield back chairs tempered the reds and golds with their Christiana brown and gold horsehair fabric, along with a mahogany 1800 Sheraton open arm chair in the same fabric. All of these textiles coordinated with the colors from the Prestwould border.

The Ladies' Parlor has a feminine touch with sewing tables and women's portraits. Courtesy Library of Virginia

Throughout the room we placed furnishings that reflected the pursuits of the ladies of that day. While gentlemen would conduct business with the Governor across the hall, ladies would be entertained with tea and casual conversation. An 1830s mahogany double lyre drop leaf sofa table with reeded legs and brass animal feet was placed in front of the sofa to display the exquisite seven piece George III antique English

A seven piece George III antique silver tea and coffee service by Paul Storr filled a mahogany double lyre drop leaf sofa table.
Courtesy Library of Virginia

silver tea and coffee service given to the house by Mrs. Leonard D. Henry. Mrs. Henry, formerly Mrs. Stewart Bryan of Richmond, was the daughter of Mrs. C. Huntley Gibson whose father was a Confederate captain from Rome, Georgia. Her gift had been a treasure in her family for several generations. Each piece is marked with London and sterling hall marks, the 1815-16 mark, profile head of George III, and the maker's mark, "P.S."

The mahogany and maple inlaid butler's secretary with cathedral doors, three brass finials and a tooled leather writing surface, circa 1800, would have been used for tea service as well as for the numerous letters written by first ladies. An 1810 Sheraton-style sewing table has a cleverly disguised hanging "basket" which would have been used to store sewing materials. This gift of Mr. and Mrs. John Curtis was paired with a Hepplewhite mahogany work table, circa 1800. A mahogany Sheraton three drawer astragal end work table, circa 1820, was placed under one of the front windows.

Very special for the Ladies' Parlor was the mahogany six-leg rectangular spinet piano. We know from an 1848 inventory that there was a piano in this room, and this piano would have been a lady's instrument. Believed to have belonged to the daughter of Governor James Barbour, it was never used at the Governor's House by the Barbours. Dating to 1830, this piano was a gift from Mrs. John Rixey of Horseshoe Farm in Rapidan, not far from the Barboursville home of Governor Barbour. An English mahogany Adams-style adjustable piano stool dating to 1790 was purchased to accompany the piano when it was acquired in 1978.

The paintings in this parlor also were chosen to reflect a feminine perspective. Attributed to Thomas Sulley, an 1830s portrait of Mary Swann once hung in the upstairs room known as the Lafayette Bedroom. This portrait and one of Mary Willing (Harrison) McGuire, on loan from the Virginia Historical Society, were hung on either side of the south window of the parlor. Since the focus of the Ladies' Parlor was to be on Virginia women, we thought these paintings were perfect representations of women of early Virginia.

Shortly before the completion of our work we were fortunate to have loaned for use at the house several paintings by Virginia artist Gari Melchers. Melchers was known for his work in his studio at his home Belmont, outside Fredericksburg. His very special portrait of his wife, Corinne, fit perfectly with our theme of Virginia women and was hung on the south wall of the Ladies' Parlor.[4]

When we had completed the Old Governor's Office and the Ladies' Parlor, we felt confident that they were treated correctly for the Federal period. A visitor would immediately feel like a guest would have felt in 1813. But the rooms were not just museum displays. They were designed to be used, and with appropriate care they would last many years.

CHAPTER 8

The Ballroom

Because the Entry Hall flows uninterrupted into the Ballroom and the view from the front door extends through these spaces to the Dining Room, it was critical to treat the first floor so that all of the open spaces blended seamlessly. This seemed to be architect Duncan Lee's intention in 1906 when he repeated the original Parris archway of the Entry Hall in the Ballroom and Dining Room doors.

The Ballroom is the most dominant room of the first floor with its columns and open expanse that extends from the north wall to the south. Yet the footprint of the two original parlors from the Parris design is still evident on either side of the columned central area leading to the Dining Room. To create unity throughout the first floor and prevent the Ballroom from becoming a cavernous space, we continued the basic gray walls and white plaster on the walls and the columns in the Ballroom that we had chosen for the Entry Hall. This created the perfect transition from the Federal-style influence of the front rooms to the Colonial Revival emphasis of the Ballroom and Dining Room. The columns are white as they would have been when they were first installed, as was the style of the Colonial Revival period. Their bases are marbleized, incorporating some of the blue from the front hallway baseboards. Duncan Lee is thought to have been influenced by the Blue Room at the White House, and so echoing this influence with blues and grays is even more appropriate in this area. Relying on the transitional features of the blue baseboards and gray walls, we chose "Chloe," an elegant blue, gray and gold wallpaper border from The Prestwould Collection by Scalamandre to adorn the ceiling line. The border's gray accents help bring the gray wall color into the Ballroom and seamlessly move from the "Janus" of the front hall. However, blue dominates the Ballroom

The Blue Room at the White House was Barbara Page's inspiration for the décor of the Ballroom. The blue, gold and gray version of "Chloe," a Scalamandre border from their Prestwould Collection, was the focal point of the design.

Courtesy Library of Virginia

as it is copied from the "Chloe" border to the window treatments that are in Abysses, a deep blue Faille Galatee taffeta with swags of Lucia Gauffe, a hammered gold silk and gold Ravinia silk taffeta. Custom handmade blue, gold, and red silk wood mold tassels adorn the edges of the swags and panels. Their design is after the treatments in the Blue Room of the White House. They are hand-draped, as are all of the draperies, by Ruth Hubbard, Kathryn Arnold, and others at the Colonial Williamsburg Drapery Studio.

The furnishings of the Ballroom presented a unique challenge to Barbara Page of Hanbury-Evans since there were no chairs in this space when we arrived in 1998. Some occasional chairs were scattered throughout the room, but other than a pair of 1810 Duncan Phyfe sofas there was no place for guests to sit. Not wanting the antique Duncan Phyfe sofas to carry the burden of guest seating, and at the same time wanting to have some comfortable seating, we added several informal upholstered chairs; we included a pair of English rolled-arm club chairs and a sofa to each side of the Ballroom. The club chairs were covered in "Linden," a pale, Flemish blue and gold wool fabric: a grapes-and-vines repeat in this fabric echoes the grapes and vines of the "Chloe" wallpaper border. We selected a marine-blue, wool Harateen fabric for the sofas. These pieces were placed in the center of the rooms to welcome guests to sit. In addition, the antique, Duncan Phyfe sofas, gifts of Mr. and Mrs. George Kaufman of Norfolk, now covered in "Hillwood," a custom gold and grotto blue silk from the Hillwood estate of Marjorie Merriweather Post, were placed off to the side. The Kaufman sofas as we came to call them would now be a focal point of the room without being the first choice of seating for guests. We wanted to protect these fine pieces from the strenuous wear Governor's House furnishings often receive.

Other changes were needed to make the Ballroom more hospitable to guests. Lighting and air conditioning were two significant issues. In order to provide adequate air conditioning during large events, we had to find some means to install a system that could be in normal operation for small groups, but put into "overdrive" for the frequent, large, lengthy receptions. The initial plan was to install the supply vents for this system into the panels that run across the width of the Ballroom at the ceiling from the front hall to the Dining Room. They would be practically unnoticed there. Unfortunately, this plan did not work because the space had to be used instead to run the electrical wiring and cables for the "smart house" system. The space was already so full that it was impossible to include the vents for the HVAC system. The best solution was to place the vents in the ceiling as close to the beams as possible. Though not invisible, they are not objectionable.

Once the matter of placing the supply vents was solved, the next question was placing HVAC system's return vents. Those needed to be hidden as well. We found a unique and completely hidden solution for this problem: The return was placed in the open space inside the pocket doors that lead from the Ballroom into the Dining Room. The doors still work, but air is drawn up into the hidden return that services both the Ballroom and Dining Room.

The smoke detection system is another example of the ingenuity of the design team. Rather than have smoke detectors that continually flash a red signal from a box on the ceiling and detract from the historic nature of the rooms, we installed a "sniffer." This system continuously breathes in the room air through a plastic tube in the base of the chandeliers. The only traces of the system are almost invisible holes in the chandeliers' bases.

While improved lighting was always an issue for the first floor, it was particularly true in the Ballroom. When originally designed by Alexander Parris, the Ballroom was basically two separate rooms that may have functioned as one large space on occasion. Each of the two rooms had an end window and two windows on its east wall, for a total of six windows in all on the back of the house. That would have served the space well. A glimpse of this original design can be seen in a photograph taken of Richmond after it was burned in the Civil War. It is a rare view of the Governor's House from the east, showing eight windows on the back of the house, four on each floor, with the bottom four being the first-floor windows of the two rear parlors.

Structural changes over the years changed the room configuration on the back of the house and lessened the available daylight in the process. Duncan Lee's opening of the two rooms into one was the first alteration of the windows. In his design, each of the back rooms lost its central back window for the door into the addition housing the new Dining Room, lessening to some extent the natural light available through the windows. Limiting natural light even more was the addition of a "breakfast porch" by Governor Price (1938–1942) onto the southeast corner of the house; this addition meant the elimination of the remaining east window in the south Ballroom; only the room's south end window remained. To maintain at least a sense of symmetry inside the house a faux window with mirrored glass was installed where this southeast window once opened to the outdoors. It continued to be treated as a window with draperies and balanced the window in the north Ballroom, but of course it no longer supplied any daylight for the now very large room.

The plan of the renovation to put an addition with handicap-accessible facilities on the northeast corner of the house was going to have yet another impact on lighting for the Ballroom. While the addition provid-

An 1865 photograph from Church Hill shows a rare glimpse of the rear of the Governor's House before the Lee Dining Room addition. The house is the light building to the right of the Capitol.   Courtesy Library of Virginia

ed long overdue handicap access and returned the exterior symmetry to the house, the northeast window of the Ballroom would no longer be available to provide natural light. The new plan made the northeast Ballroom window a door leading into the new addition. Though it still would be treated like a window with draperies like the mirrored window of the south Ballroom, this new door would not even provide the reflected light of a mirror. Now there were no windows on the east walls of the Ballroom where there had originally been four. The only sources of natural light for this large room were the two windows at either end of the room. The chandeliers, gifts of the Gottwald family of Richmond, could not provide sufficient light for the space in this new configuration. In order to address the lighting problem, while the chandeliers were removed during the construction for cleaning, they were rewired to add a second tier of candles. Bill and Mary Ellen Toombs of Toombs Electrical in Richmond removed each

John Paul Hanbury, center, talks with Bill and Mary Ellen Toombs about period light fixtures at the Governor's House. The Toombs refurbished and added a tier of candles to the Ballroom fixtures to provide more light.   Courtesy DHR

70   Restoring the Virginia Governor's House

prism and hand cleaned them. These sparkling crystals now reflect the light from two tiers of candles and help make up for some of the light from the lost windows.

Our treatment of the parquet floors completed the transition to this Colonial Revival room. Oriental carpets were customary in formal spaces of early 20th century homes and were already present in the Governor's House Ballroom. Though the existing rugs were somewhat small for the spaces, they did work with the color scheme and we decided to keep the rugs where they were. The use of these Orientals had been anticipated by using loose-laid Brussels carpets in the Entry Hall so there would not be an abrupt change in style.

Ballroom Furnishings

With the addition of new, comfortable seating, the Ballroom was ready to greet the large volume of guests who are regularly entertained at the Governor's House. These pieces gave a sense of scale to the rooms and kept them from being cold, open areas. Also used to give scale to the room was the large circa 1800 mahogany butler's secretary placed at the entry from the Ballroom to the new addition. The size of this piece was appropriate for the room, and we used it to display many of the unique pieces of the ceramic collection. This secretary has an interesting history, and a handwritten letter by its donor, Mr. John J. Williams, details the life of this piece and its origins in Amherst County. We placed a pair of Hepplewhite

English rolled-arm club chairs and a sofa were added to give scale to the room as well as provide comfortable seating for guests.

Courtesy Library of Virginia

Ruth Hubbard of the Colonial Williamsburg Design Studio hand-sewed the deep blue taffeta and hammered gold silk panels and swags of the Ballroom.
Courtesy Library of Virginia

mahogany inlaid demilune tables on either side of the fireplace. These tables, attributed to Christian Beur of Churchville, circa 1780, are inlaid with rectangular panels of checkered borders and undulating fan quadrants flanked by burl veneered inlaid panels on the stiles. The legs have a rare bulb and diamond inlay. They were purchased with a gift by Mr. and Mrs. Gerald Halpin of Fairfax County. Other tables dating to the early 19th century were used throughout the room as well.

Balancing the butler's secretary in the south Ballroom was a mahogany Steinway grand piano used to provide background music for receptions and dinners. Still used today, this piano, manufactured April 8, 1926, is said to have been purchased by Governor Harry Byrd after fire destroyed much of the first floor. Part of house lore is the tale that Governor Byrd sold the state limousine to pay for the piano. Many stories such as this have been told again and again about the House and its occupants and are part of the fascination that Virginians have with their Governor's home.

Much thought was given to the paintings that were used in the ballrooms. Over the identical mantels of both areas, we hung a pair of 18th century gold leaf Adam-style wall mirrors with column side rails crowned with floral scroll open gesso work. Virginia and its scenery and history are the focus of the other paintings that we chose for the Ballroom. On the walls next to the fireplaces were landscape paintings owned by the Governor's House. In the north Ballroom were landscape scenes from some of Virginia's beautiful rivers: "The St. James River," an oil on canvas mounted on board, by A. Davidson; "Jackson's River," a gilt-framed oil on canvas by Russell Smith; and "Arch of Sandstone on the Potomac River," an oil on wood panel also by Smith. In the south Ballroom were "Callahans Meadow, Virginia," a gold-leaf framed oil on canvas by Smith; and "James River, Virginia 1860," a gilt-framed oil on canvas attributed to David Johnson, circa 1860.[1]

The major emphasis on paintings in the Ballroom, however, was on the walls on both sides of the entrance to the Dining Room. As one enters from the front hall, these large spaces immediately come into view, along with the central wall in the Dining Room. In this vista, we decided to hint at the history of Virginia from its earliest days to the 20th century. In the Dining Room, the

Virginian Nancy Viscountess Astor, C. H., gave a portrait of Queen Elizabeth I to the Commonwealth as a reminder that women can "add to a country's greatness even if they don't happen to be mothers!"
Courtesy Library of Virginia

72 Restoring the Virginia Governor's House

main focus of this expanse, we hung the portrait of Queen Elizabeth I, the English queen for whom Virginia is named. Perhaps the most valuable piece of the Commonwealth's art collection, it was a gift from Nancy Viscountess Astor, C. H., a Virginian by birth. We proudly showcased it to herald the arrival of 2007, the 400th anniversary of the founding of Virginia, the oldest permanently occupied English colony in the New World. On the wall in the north Ballroom, we hung a gold-leaf framed oil on canvas portrait entitled, "Alexander Spotswood, 1676–1740," by Charles Bridges. On loan from the Library of Virginia, this painting summons the image of early Virginia and its dramatic westward expansion by the colonial Governor Spotswood and his Knights of the Golden Horseshoe. On the wall in the south Ballroom we placed an oil on canvas portrait of Nancy Viscountess Astor by James Gunn. Though she moved to England and spent her adult life in London, Nancy Astor was proud of her Virginia birth, and as the first woman to serve as a member of the British House of Commons, it seemed appropriate that her portrait be displayed to represent the forward-looking progress of Virginia in the 20th century.

To preserve the new fabrics of the furniture in the Ballroom we had slipcovers made for the hot summer months.

The Battleship USS Virginia was commissioned in 1906, the same year that Duncan Lee added the formal dining room to the Governor's House. The silver, including its punch bowl with images of seven of the eight Virginians who served as President, was returned to the Dining Room from display cases in the side halls. The silver service and candle sticks were placed on the Hepplewhite sideboard beneath the restored Queen Elizabeth portrait.

Courtesy Library of Virginia

74 Restoring the Virginia Governor's House

CHAPTER 9

The Dining Room and Breakfast Room

The first floor room that makes one of the grandest impressions on visitors is the Dining Room. Guests, whether casual visitors to Capitol Square or dinner guests seated at the long, 32-place table, remark on its understated elegance. Duncan Lee, commissioned at the beginning of the administration of Governor Claude Swanson in 1906, designed the oval-shaped room that he housed in an octagonal building to maximize the limited space on the hilltop at the rear of the house. This shape also gave corners that allowed for built in cabinets for china storage and access to pantries as well as a stairway to the basement. Lee's inspiration for this room was the Blue Room at the White House, and he sought to incorporate elements of the Colonial Revival period in this room as he had in his newly-designed Ballroom. A great arched doorway, copied from the Parris Entry Hall, welcomes guests to the dining area. In its original design the room had four windows, one window on each of the north and south ends of the oval, and two other windows on either side of a manteled fireplace in the center of the east façade. This fireplace faced the front door and was at the end of Lee's central hallway. The Dining Room was originally only one story and stood alone across the back of the structure.

The Duncan Lee design did not last long, however. In 1914 Governor Stuart added a second floor over the Dining Room in order to have more bedrooms. At that time, then former Governor Montague let Stuart know his dislike of the size and design of the Lee Dining Room (see page 17) and urged him not to make similar mistakes in the work he was getting ready to do on the second floor. Stuart went forward with his changes despite Governor Montague's opinion. In 1926 Governor Harry Byrd, seeming to agree with

The State Seal and a tobacco braid are highlights of the specially loomed Dining Room carpet. The Queen Elizabeth I portrait hung in the position of honor over the Hepplewhite sideboard.

Courtesy Library of Virginia

Montague that the room lacked wall space for appropriate furnishings, removed the grand fireplace on the east wall. This created a long wall space that could be used for a sideboard.[1]

Because of its large size, the Dining Room can be overwhelming for day-to-day family dining; we found it awkward for the four of us to eat in such a cavernous space. It is reported that Governor Price in the 1930s not only did not enjoy living in the house, but particularly did not like eating in this very large, formal room. He had a porch built on the southeast corner of the room and used this smaller space to eat breakfast. This is the addition that blocked the southeastern window of the Ballroom, and led to the mirrored window being added in its place. In the 1940s Governor William Tuck had the porch glassed in, and in 1954 the porch was made into a formal addition with a second story. It turned the "dining porch" into a small, enclosed Breakfast Room and added a paneled den to the second floor living quarters. As a result, there is now a small, more intimate Breakfast Room, appropriate for family meals or a governor's small business luncheons.

On first glance prior to the 1998 renovation, the Dining Room appeared to be in good condition and seemingly in need of only minimal attention. In the prior administration of George Allen, a complete set of dining room chairs, 32 in all, had been commissioned. The burgundy drapes and the Stark carpet had also been added.

The carpet had been a special project of the Citizens Advisory Committee. B. Lynn Warren, a member of the CAC, collaborated with Paige Goodman, Head of the Art Department at Stark, to design this 30' by 90' oval rug to include various symbols of Virginia. Completed in a special random tip weave to give an aged look, the Virginia State Seal is the focus along the outside border. Trailing alongside the seal are the state shell (Chesapecten jeffersonius), dogwood flowers and a tobacco braid, all representing Virginia's natural heritage. However, after viewing the beautiful furniture, draperies, and this handsome rug, we soon realized that the room in fact did have significant needs.

Temperature control was always the most overriding issue throughout the house. This was no exception in the Dining Room. Spoiling the beautiful décor were the "Sunday school" air handlers beneath each of the windows. State of the art in the 1950s when they were added by Governor John S. Battle, these painted metal handlers

Fred Ecker of Tidewater Preservation, Inc., made detailed observations of the damage done to the parquet floors by the air conditioning system.
Courtesy DHR

were now rusting and had paint popping off. But it wasn't just the look of the metal units that was the issue. More important was the damage that each of the registers was causing in the room. When it was hot and the air conditioning was on, the units condensed moisture and water streamed across the parquet flooring to the carpet; they cooled very little, too. The new carpet was becoming stained on the back from the puddles that formed, and we feared that eventually the rug would mildew, fade or rot. The parquet floors were also being damaged by the pooling water. The deterioration done to the walls behind the air conditioning units was equally serious as the damage to the floors. The walls were not only stained, but in places were rotting, one to the point where there was a complete hole in the wainscoting.

The small Breakfast Room had only minor problems, mostly ones of décor. When first added, this room had been papered with lovely, hand painted wall covering by the Gracie Company. Over time this fabric had become faded from the intense sunlight that fills this room all day. An attempt had been made by Governor Douglas Wilder's daughter to repaint portions of this, and while it was well done and preserved the paper for some time, it had not been completed and there were partially painted panels interspersed with finished ones. By the time of our arrival, none were the vibrant colors of the original, however, and we decided that, since the paper had already been modified, repapering the room with new Gracie paper was the best way to proceed.

Because of the work done by the Allen administration, the furnishings for the Dining Room were basically complete. We kept everything that we could and the rug and draperies that had been put in place were still appropriate with the other choices we had made on the first floor. The Hepplewhite bellflower sideboard, a gift of Nancy Chapman Wallomer, kept its place along the east wall its unusual triple serpentine front makes it a rare piece and among the most treasured in the house. The object of our renovation was not to change things just to change them; we had a reason for every choice that we made, most often based on research. The CAC and newly formed Foundation were kept informed of our choices because they would be the integral part in funding and maintaining the decorative elements of the restoration.

One of the major changes we made involving the Dining Room was the decision to openly display the silver from the USS Battleship Virginia here. This silver had been commissioned by the General Assembly in 1906 to celebrate the recently christened Battleship Virginia. After moving from the USS Virginia to the USS Richmond to the USS Roanoke as the ships were decommissioned, the silver had been placed into storage where it was located by First Lady Josephine Almond. Knowing that other states had their silver, with determination–and $165 C.O.D. charges from husband's pocket–she worked to have this silver service returned to the Commonwealth. When we arrived at the House, the silver was on display in cases built into the doors of the Old Governor's Office and Ladies' Parlor. As mentioned in Chapter 7, these cases were poorly lit, and silver on the lower shelves was difficult to see. Clearly, visitors could not enjoy this treasure as it should be. Moreover, we had decided to return the doors to the parlors, so a new arrangement for displaying the silver had to be found. We believed that the 1906 creation date of both the silver and the Dining Room made the Dining Room an appropriate choice for the silver's presentation.

Candlesticks and other pieces were used on side tables, dining table, and on the Hepplewhite sideboard. The magnificent punch bowl, encircled with the portraits of seven of Virginia's eight presidents–Woodrow Wilson had not been president by the time of the creation of the silver–was placed in the center of the Ballroom so that visitors could walk completely around it and see it from all sides. It could now be viewed in its entirety as it deserved.

Special Projects of the Dining Room

The oval shape of the Lee Dining Room created special preservation issues for the Tidewater Preservation team in their restoration of the parquet floors and wainscoting. The perimeter of the floor conformed to the oval shape of the room, and the parquet had to be specially prepared to fit this shape. Oak patches salvaged from the first floor side halls were fitted to the damaged areas and through a special process were radiused to fit the curved shape of the floor. As in the front parlors, the HVAC vents were disguised in the wainscot, much of which had to be replaced because of the significant moisture damage from the old air conditioning units.

In the arched doorway between the Ballroom and Dining Room were a pocket door and the entrance for the small elevator that ran from the basement to the second floor. Though small, the elevator could be used to bring items up from the Kitchen to the Dining Room or Breakfast Room. When the decision was made to build a new wing to provide accessibility and more space, there was no discussion of losing the arch or the pocket doors, but there was no longer any need for this original elevator which had significant maintenance issues. Plans were made to eliminate the elevator and gain more space on each floor. However, as demolition of the shaft proceeded, we noticed one day that the floor of the rooms over the Dining Room was in part supported by the shaft beams of the elevator. Removing them would most certainly cause a collapse of the floor. Despite our pre-construction efforts had we hit the unforeseen, schedule-busting snag? We immediately stopped the demolition and made new plans for the elevator shaft.

Storage for the leaves of the dining room table had always been difficult. The leaves were large and heavy and needed special care to prevent scratching and scarring the surface. The elevator shaft, no longer on the schedule to be removed, provided an ideal location to build storage racks for the table leaves. The shaft was just deep enough to build supports to hold the individual table pieces, and its convenient location made it a perfect solution for this need. What serendipity!

The Breakfast Room

One of my favorite rooms in the house was the Breakfast Room. On the southeast end of the Dining Room overlooking the beautiful Gillette Garden, this room has a bright, airy atmosphere. The Gracie Company wallpaper, original to the room, had been a superb selection. Even in its faded condition its birds and floral garlands made you feel almost like you were in the garden. But mostly, it was the human scale of the room that was so appealing. After coming through the vast, formal rooms of the Ballroom and Dining Room, going into the Breakfast Room was like going home. Keeping this beautiful normalcy was our primary goal for the Breakfast Room. Continuing to use Gracie wallpaper in the room was the perfect way to achieve this goal.

Custom made, Gracie paper can be matched exactly to a color scheme. This feature enabled us to use a similar design on the paper but update its colors to the palette that we were using throughout the first floor rooms. The background color was matched to the gray that we had used in the front parlors and Ballroom, thus unifying the entire floor's décor.

When we began to hang the new paper, the first attempt showed quickly that standard methods for hanging paper did not work with these delicate, hand-screened sheets. A search was launched to find someone experienced in

A clear line can be seen on the Gracie wallpaper in the Breakfast Room. The strong sunlight in the room had faded much of the paper.
Courtesy DHR

applying Gracie paper. Luckily, an experienced hanger was found who was chosen and arrived to start this delicate task. And, if you have ever hung wallpaper yourself in a small room, you know he was going to have a difficult enough time in the confined space he had to work, even if he were using ordinary paper. When I returned from school one day, I found him busily at work, attired in a smock and beret. Taking his assignment to heart, he told me, "This is not wallpaper, it is art." His work took several days, even for this small space. Handling it with that kind of respect, as well as a slow and methodical pace, were his keys to a successful job.

The Breakfast Room was completed with the addition of a Waterford chandelier from our friend, crime-novelist Patricia Cornwell. Though somewhat smaller than other chandeliers in the house, it was the perfect scale for this more personal space, and its delicate, crystal prisms reflected an abundance of light from the windows.

Juxtaposed to each other, the Dining Room and Breakfast Room illustrate to me the paradox of living in the Governor's House. Though both rooms are elegant to be sure, they each invoke the different paths that life takes when one resides there. The Dining Room, with its lavish silver display and carpet symbolic of Virginia's heritage, exemplify the central role of the house in the life of the Commonwealth as well as the role of the Governor's family in that life. Its size, large to accommodate the crowds that attend the many state functions, reflects its significance. On the other hand, the Breakfast Room is small and like a retreat from the daily bustle of Capitol Square. Its view of the garden belies its real location in the middle of the city. But most of all, the Breakfast Room harkens back to the inescapable fact that the house is a family's residence and that their lives continue on a personal level alongside the activities of the state. Neither room nor role is more important.

CHAPTER 10

The First Family's Living Quarters

Privacy is always the first luxury of life that members of the first family lose as they move into the Governor's House. House staff members are eager to help them move into their new quarters, the Executive Protection Unit members are ever present, and ready to escort them to their destinations and, with the General Assembly already in session, guests at almost nightly receptions fill the downstairs.

In the Governor's House before the renovation, this loss of privacy was accentuated by the dual staircases from the first floor that opened directly into the family's "private" living quarters. When we arrived in 1998, these staircases opened into a series of small, connected rooms that, because of their configuration, were often difficult to use. Also, at the head of the stairs was a large open space known as the Capitol Room that ushered people into the remaining historic rooms of the second floor.

The only historic spaces remaining on the second floor were the rooms along the front of the house overlooking

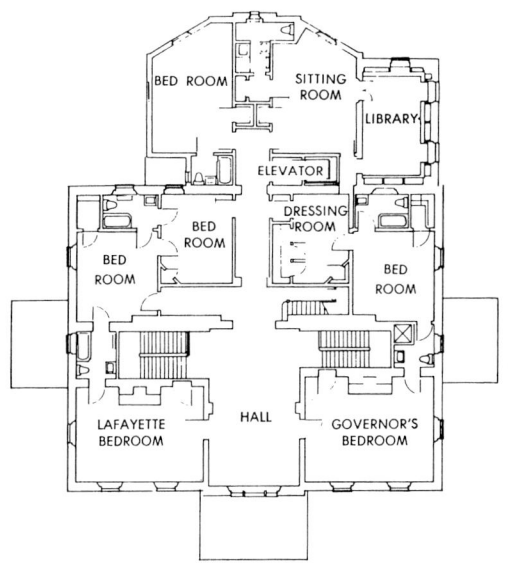

Second floor plan

Though called by different names, with minor changes the rooms on this floor plan were essentially the layout of the living quarters at the time of the renovation.

Capitol Square. Flanking the Capitol Room on its north side was the Lafayette Bedroom. On the Capitol Room's south side was another large room that had been used in various ways over the years. Both of these rooms retained their original symmetrical design and fireplaces. Legend has it that Lafayette changed his clothes on a visit to Richmond in the north room, though it was sometime after his visit that the room received his name. This room was still treated as a bedroom and in its north corner was a bathroom that was shared with an adjoining small bedroom.

The corresponding room on the south front of the house had been used in various ways by different administrations—as a bedroom by some, as a living room by others, and by Jim as a personal office. In its southeast corner a door led into a kitchenette that connected to a small room that had been used as a dining room. The kitchenette had a stove that did not work and had no hood and only a small refrigerator.

On its east end at the head of the steps, the Capitol Room opened through double doors into a broad, central hall that led directly to the Governor's bedroom, which was situated at the back of the house over the Lee Dining Room. There were numerous rooms off of this hall, none of which was original to the design of the house but had been added over the years by various administrations.

Jim's office on the southwest corner opened in the rear into the small kitchenette on the second floor.   Courtesy DHR

As you stepped beyond the doors from the Capitol Room into this central hall, there were two narrow hallways which led to each side of the house. One hall went south to the room that had been used as a dining room and was connected by the kitchenette to the original room on the front of the house. The other hall went north to the small bedroom that was connected by the walk-through bathroom to the Lafayette Bedroom.

Continuing down the central hall one came to a series of small rooms. The room on the south was the Governor's Dressing Room. It was a square room with built-in dressers and it had a very large Nautilus machine in the center of the floor. The Dressing Room had multiple doors. As you entered from the hall door, a door on your left led to a small area with an entrance to the second floor library and to the Governor's bedroom. Opposite the door from the hall was a door to a very small, paneled bathroom. The bathroom was small with the toilet directly in front of the door and a stall shower and sink along the side wall. Next to the bathroom door was a door to the small dining room. From his

The governor's Dressing Room was a room full of doors into various spaces – a closet, a bathroom, the hall, the Breakfast Room and a hallway to the master bedroom and library.
Courtesy DHR

Dressing Room the Governor could go to his bedroom and library, the Dining Room, his bathroom, or the main hall–all through different doors!

Past the Dressing Room at the end of the central hall on the south was the door to the elevator, providing access to the first floor and basement. Because there was no kitchen in the living quarters, when the family ate upstairs the meal had to be brought on the elevator from the basement.

Finally, on the north side of the central hall, directly across from the Governor's Dressing Room, was a small bedroom and bath. This bedroom was connected to the other small bedroom on the north side of the house, with a shared the bathroom.

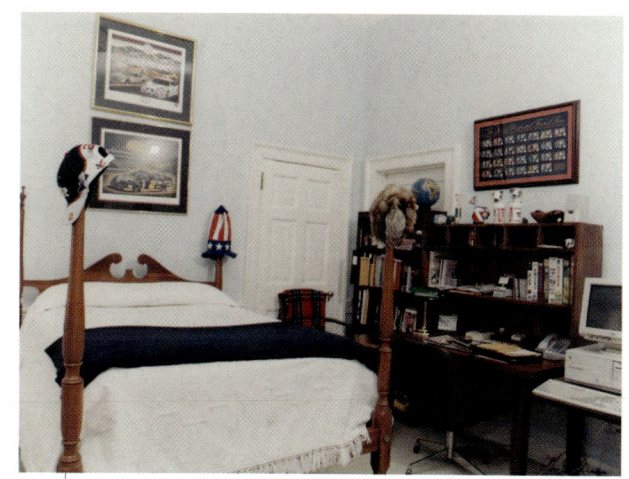

Like so many of the second floor rooms, this bedroom had multiple doors and little wall space for furniture.

Courtesy DHR

At the end of the central hall, situated over a portion of the Lee Dining Room, was the Governor's bedroom suite. The north end area of the suite was the First Lady's Dressing Room. It was a small space including a bathroom. The bathroom was very elegant with marble floors and lovely décor. Because the dressing area was situated over the end of the oval Dining Room, its space was small and irregular in shape.

The Governor's bedroom was over the central part of the Lee Dining Room. This part of the suite was spacious, with room for a large wardrobe containing a television, a large poster bed, two wing chairs and a tea table. At the south end of the bedroom was the entrance to the paneled library that had been added in 1958 over the small Breakfast Room on the south end of the Dining Room. Next to the library was a door to the Governor's Dressing Room.

By 1998 the second floor living quarters were a series of connected spaces that were often difficult to use. The paneled den, a comfortable space where the family could have met with guests, could be reached only through the Governor's bedroom or his Dressing Room. As we quickly discovered, most food had to be brought from the basement to the second floor on the one person elevator, practically in the middle of the family's bedroom quarters. Our primary goal in the restoration of the second floor was to create accommodations that would give the first family a private, comfortable living space and a refuge from the bustle of Capitol Square. But we also wanted rooms, like the library, where the family should be able to welcome guests, to be reachable without going through private areas.

Though the commitment was made to keep the front three rooms of the second floor true to their original appearance, we felt that the previously altered space on the back of the house could be used to better advantage. A new design by John Paul Hanbury accomplished this goal by creating a dual space on the second floor. The front three rooms remained as they were. Very little work was needed in the Capitol Room, and only small changes were made in the other two front rooms. In the south room the kitchenette that had been a walk-through to the dining room was changed to a full bathroom and the walk-through closed. That made this room useful for many possibilities–family room, bedroom or office.

The structure of the Lafayette Bedroom was not changed at all, and we updated the bathroom with new fixtures. The bathroom continued to be a conduit from the front of the house to the back, and it is the

Ashton pitches in during the demolition of the second floor. The entire floor from the stairwells east was removed.
Courtesy DHR

only direct connection from the historic front of the house to the newly configured rear. The bathroom is used not only by the Lafayette Bedroom, but because of a back door it can be used by people who are in the family quarters.

At the double doors from the Capitol Room, we began a whole new living space. Around and within a circular shaped corridor that runs from the double doors are rooms designed for family living. While Hanbury had ideas about how to use each room, in the end each family chooses how the space best accommodates its needs.

Included in the family area is a room designed to be a sitting area for the family. It has a door that enters the bathroom adjoining the Lafayette Room. It also has large, built in cabinets for a television and music system, and extra shelves for bookcases.

Knowing that families would have their own preferences about décor, when selecting the fabrics and color scheme for this room, we took a conservative approach, hoping that these basics could be used with many combinations. A black and taupe Brunschwig & Fils fabric Suki Woven pattern covered two club chairs, with a complementary chair in charcoal on cream West Indies Toile also by Brunschwig & Fils. An ottoman in a Leopard pattern by Westgate/Payne could be used with any of the chairs. Along the north wall of the room there was a sofa covered in beige Woodland Chenille by Bailey and Griffin. We continued the neutral theme of the family room by using the West Indies Toile pattern of the club chair in the window treatment.

The family room connects to the area of the new addition to the building. The new accessible elevator opens into this area. The elevator doors were faux-finished to resemble panel doors to try to give a homier feel to the space.

The northeast addition provided space for a full kitchen for the family in their living quarters for the first time. One of the major drawbacks of the Governor's House for a family had always been its lack of a true Kitchen anywhere but in the basement. Now there was room for the family to have a state of the art kitchen with a stove and oven, a combination halogen/microwave oven, a sink and dishwasher and a full-sized refrigerator. The space was even large enough to put a table and four chairs if some members of the family chose to dine there. Again we chose neutral colors for this space. The large windows in the Kitchen were treated with a cream background, floral, Schumacher pattern called Studio Botanico.

Continuing in the circle are the bedroom and the dressing rooms and baths for the Governor and First Lady. The Governor's bathroom is completely accessible, from Dressing Room to shower. Though designed to be the Governor's room, it could accommodate anyone with special needs. The First Lady's area has a Dressing Room with a connected bath with both tub and shower.

The window treatments in the Governor's bedroom were a Travers Tulip Crewel in rose and blue tones, again a neutral choice. The dressing room spaces of the Governor and First Lady each had a basic, Viscount Stripe Brunschwig and Fils wallpaper pattern in white on eggshell. For the First Lady's bathroom, a very private space on the interior of the living quarters, we chose a coral Scalamandre wall covering.

Completing the circular corridor were doors to a small bedroom and bathroom, the doorway to the existing paneled den, and finally a door to a bedroom and bathroom on the south side of the house. Beyond this last room is the turn to go back to the beginning of the circle at the double doors.

We gave these two smaller bedrooms wall coverings by Brunschwig & Fils, a Courtney Striae pattern, midnight blue in one room and pine green in the other. To brighten the blue room we used a whimsical, Scalamandre crewel fabric with a white background and blue figures in window length draperies. We used similar window length draperies in the green bedroom made from a Bailey and Griffin fabric in burgundy and a complementary green.

We treated the paneled den, a warm, beautiful space overlooking the Gillette Garden in the style of an English country house. We placed a classic, walnut-glazed leather sofa along the one free wall space which we covered in a yellow Washan Jute wall covering by Schumacher. Two club chairs covered in the Scalamandre fabric Edwin Covey, had a muted floral pattern with a bevy of quail as the focal element. Not wanting to obscure the view to the garden we used a minimal window treatment in a taupe Schumacher fabric called Luminescence.

The Lafayette Bedroom

As part of the original Parris plan of the house, we gave the Lafayette Bedroom the same attention to historic décor as we had given the first floor. Because of the story of Lafayette using the room as a bedroom, because the room had its own bath and because other space had been provided for family living, we decided to leave the room as a bedroom and emphasize its historical significance.

The walls in the Lafayette room received some of the most special attention in the project. When removing walls in the basement for its reconfiguration, we discovered remnants of wall covering that was dated by Colonial Williamsburg to the 1840s. Because of its style and location, we believed that it could have been the wallpaper used by "Extra Billy" Smith when the dining room was moved to the basement in 1846. We decided to have this wall covering and its accompanying Greek key border reproduced and used in the Lafayette Bedroom. Barbara Page of Hanbury Evans designed window treatments and bed hangings based on those in George Washington's bedroom at Mount Vernon. John Paul Hanbury had a tester specially made for the bed. Ruth Hubbard and her team from Colonial Williamsburg hand sewed new Richmond white dimity cloth for the window and bed treatments in this room. The bed hangings were finished on both sides so that even inside the tester there was a hand-sewn panel around the top. The side panels could be closed, and with the result was so special that it was selected in March 2000 Architectural Digest as a part of their article on the restoration on this room. Unfortunately much of the work done in this room has been lost. The window treatments and bed hangings were used in a child's room in a later administration and they were damaged beyond repair when an attempt was made to wash them.

The Lafayette Bedroom was one of the most detailed rooms of the restoration. The bed treatment was handmade with detail work inside and outside the tester and panels that completely closed. The wallpaper and border were reproduced from paper dated to the 1840s that was found in the basement demolition.

Courtesy Library of Virginia

Though none of the rooms on the second floor of the house have functions absolutely demanded for their use, for our time there the results on this floor produced a double outcome. The front of the house now could take advantage of its historic nature without imposing on the family's privacy. Jim set up a working office in the south front room and was able to have meetings and do official work without affecting our private space. Guests could be shown the Lafayette Bedroom on special occasions, and it could even be used as a guest bedroom. But in the rear of the house we had a real, private living area. For the first time there was a complete kitchen where food could be stored and cooked and meals eaten. This was especially nice for our two children, who were usually not invited to dinners downstairs and needed a place of their own to eat. Governors now had a full Dressing Room and a reliable bathroom with an accessible shower. They were no longer off of the main hall. And the library, so very special to us for our books and computer and even a television, had its own doorway from the hall. The joint public, private life a governor's family is expected to lead can now be accomplished with a measure of comfort and of feeling at home.

CHAPTER 11

The Basement

While most visitors to the Governor's House would say that the first floor, with its understated elegance, bears the work load of the house, those who have spent any time there, know that the real heart of the building is the basement. In it are the areas where the staff do all of the work of the house including security, catering and daily meals, laundry and housekeeping, guest services, and general household management. Also, the First Lady can choose to use room here for her office and activities. Moreover, storage space is needed for food, linens, china, office equipment, and general household items. The basement level must provide the specialized spaces for all of these different functions.

Of all the floors at the Governor's House, the basement is the one that I have the most difficulty describing. As originally constructed, it appears to have had an unusual layout, and the various ways in which it has been used over the years have added to its complexity. Moreover, like the first floor, there are stories that have been passed down about how the basement was used, and while some of our discoveries supported these stories, other finds just created more questions. To try to bring some clarity, I'll discuss how the floor was laid out and used when we arrived, what we discovered about the early building as construction proceeded, and finally the results of our efforts to make the floor more efficient.

The Basement Layout on Our Arrival

The basement of the Governor's House is not a completely underground floor as some may think when they hear the word basement. There are in fact ground level windows around the base of the house, no

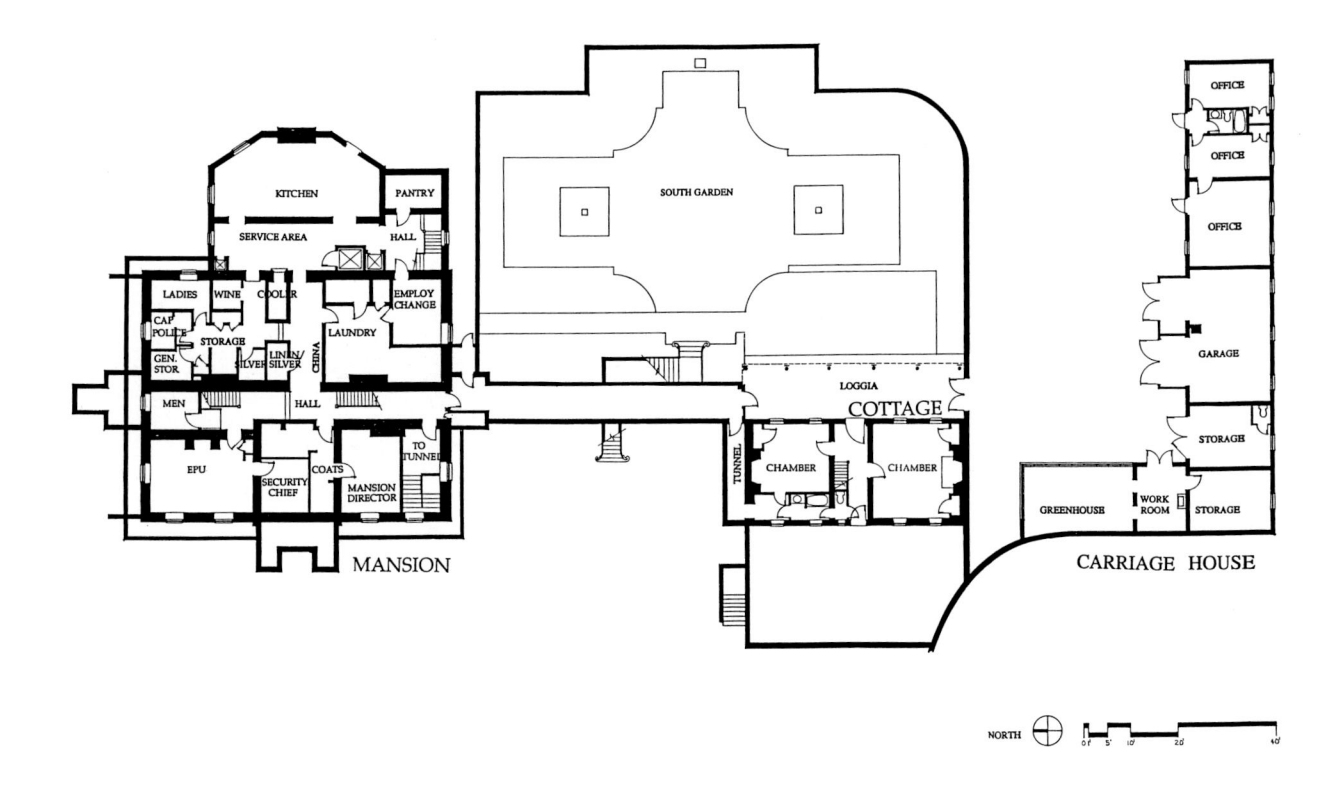

The basement floor plan as it existed at the beginning of the project, was a confused arrangement of rooms on different levels. The space was totally reconfigured. The greenhouse and work room attached to the Carriage House were demolished to make room for a new gate into the compound.

doubt the chief method of lighting for a floor expected to be used in the early days before electricity. Over time some of the windows had been shortened and some, like the one in the men's room under the north staircase, even covered over; it is beneath the portico that was added to the side entrance.

When we moved in, the approximately 4000 square foot basement was arranged on two levels, with small steps between these levels. Stairs led down from the north and south hallways of the first floor with the north stairway being the most frequently used. There were three offices on the front of the house (the west side) at the foot of these stairs. The Executive Protection Unit (EPU) used the room on the northwest corner as their administrative center. This center had very low ceilings, so low in fact that some of the troopers had difficulty standing upright. At its south end there was a separate office for Ron Watkins, Chief of Security. Outside the main door to the EPU center, situated beneath the north staircase, was a men's restroom which I was told was a fairly Spartan facility.

The EPU area and the restroom were on a higher level than the other offices on this side of the house. There were two small steps, separate from the main staircase, to get down to the lower floor level of those offices. On this lower level was the entrance to the rooms used by House Director, Donna Case. Her assistant, Amy Finch, who arranged and kept the schedule of house tours, managed the tour docent program, and assisted the Director in event planning and management had her desk at the doorway. Amy's space was also used as a coat closet for large events. At the back of this suite was the door into Donna's office. On the southwest corner of the house, it had small, ground level windows which were matched by ground level windows in the EPU office.

There was a hallway that led south to the garden and Cottage between the director's office and the south staircase from the first floor. On the west wall of this hall was an entrance to the Capitol Square tunnels, an underground system of passages leading to various buildings in and around Capitol Square. These passages also accommodate wiring, plumbing, and heating needs.

On the south side of the house, beyond the entrance to the tunnels, was a door that opened to a passageway beneath the walkway from the main house to the Cottage. This passage, about 55 feet long, had been added in 1846 as a latticed walkway to what was then the kitchen. Tunnel-like since it was enclosed in 1955, at its end a door opened directly into the loggia of the Cottage. But just before the door outside was a short hall on the right. This hall quickly turned left and emerged inside the back hall of the first floor of the Cottage.

On the east side of the basement was the Kitchen, an oval-shaped space that was situated beneath the Duncan Lee Dining Room added in 1906. The Kitchen was divided by a partition across the room that created two separate areas. On the west side of the partition was a service area with a residential sized dishwasher, built-in storage cabinets for china, the entrance to the elevator, a walk-in refrigerator, and desks for the chef and his *sous* chef beneath a south wall staircase to the first floor dining area. Behind the elevator was the entrance to a room used at different times as an office and sometimes a changing room for the staff, but its sequestered location made it inconvenient for much use.

On the east side of the partition was the working kitchen, which was filled in the center with two islands for pot and pan storage and counter space for food preparation. Along the east wall was an exit outside, a large electric stove and oven, sinks, and more counter space. There were windows over the counters and sink, giving some natural light to this area. To be sure, the Kitchen had adequate work space, but over the years it had become inefficiently arranged, and storage was always an issue.

Connecting the Director's office, EPU offices, and the Kitchen was a corridor in the middle of the basement that ran west to east. On either side of this corridor were rooms with storage closets along the walls. On the north side of the corridor was a hall with a step up into a little group of rooms. These rooms, situated under the north Ballroom, were used for a variety of purposes. There was an office at the end of the hall with storage areas lining the hall. There was a very small room, only about 4' by 7', for the Capitol police. Also in this area was

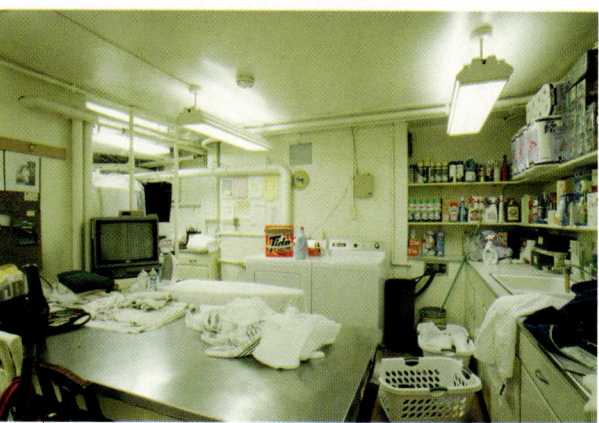

TOP: *A scullery adjoining the Kitchen had two residential size dishwashers that had to serve for functions of all sizes.*
BOTTOM: *The Laundry Room had a large table for work space.*
Courtesy DHR

a ladies' bathroom. Another narrow hallway turned right and led to the Kitchen. Along this hallway was a handsomely paneled wine closet. Beyond the wine closet was a step down from this group of rooms into the service area of the Kitchen.

On the south side of the central corridor was the door to the laundry, a large room about 16' by 22' used for a variety of functions. In addition to having a washer, dryer, and ironing board, the Laundry Room was used as storage for linens, silver, and china. The works of the elevator were also in a utility closet here.

The complexity of this floor was matched by its state of disrepair and inaccessibility. Lighting and other utilities were dated and inefficient. The plaster was blistered and paint was peeling because the bricks of the foundation wicked water that damaged the walls. In addition to age, the washer, dryer, and dishwashers were all just family-sized, and the size and frequency of events at the house had strained their capacity. Even the walk-in refrigerator did not cool enough to keep milk more than a few days.

One of the worst features of the basement was that it was not handicap accessible. It was almost impossible for someone in a wheelchair to get down to the basement. The staircases from the main first floor hall were narrow and steep, and carrying someone down these stairs would have been unsafe. The elevator was not an option either, because it was not big enough to accommodate a wheelchair. Finally, even if someone entered the basement through the garden, the floor was difficult to maneuver because of the multiple levels throughout that required going up and down small steps.

Plans for Redesigning

The plan to redesign the basement had to be done simultaneously with that of the first floor to produce the optimal result. Since there was very little historic structure left in the basement, the systems of the first

FROM LEFT: *Donna Case, Mark Herndon, John Paul Hanbury, Sam Daniel and Tutti Townes discuss the needs of the household staff in order to design a basement that would function efficiently.* Courtesy Library of Virginia

floor, HVAC, electrical, and plumbing, were all to be incorporated from the basement level as much as possible to prevent the loss of historic building fabric on the first floor. Moreover, a variety of activities that occur at the house are choreographed from the basement and this required the development of specialized centers for the staff.

What many don't realize is that the Governor's House is not just the residence of the First Family. In addition, it is a center for Economic Development, a tourist venue (during our stay, open on almost a daily basis during the week), a reception hall for myriad official events at the invitation of the Governor and First Lady, a police station, a catering facility, a laundry, and an office complex for the house staff. Each of these activities creates special demands on the house. The staff was invaluable in giving their guidance as to changes to the basement that would make all of these functions work more smoothly and which would ultimately lead to better care of the historic first floor.

The design team met with those whose operations were centered in the basement in order to understand their needs. EPU Director Ron Watkins wanted a state of the art security system, including cameras, alarms, smoke detectors, and fire alarms. Chef Mark Herndon used his training at the Culinary Institute of America to help develop a state of the art kitchen so that luncheons, parties, banquets, and everyday dining could be provided in house with greater efficiency. House Director Donna Case, and Head of the Household Staff, Martin "Tutti" Townes, gave us great insight as to the general needs of the staff. Maintenance of silver, china, and linens which required both storage and work space, and convenient access to get these items to the first and second floors, were the focus of their discussions. In addition to these basic staff needs, Donna and Tutti were most instructive as to the needs of guests. For example, the basement could provide the space for additional restroom facilities which they deemed inadequate.

One of the first decisions was to bring the floor to one level, making it accessible for the first time. Ridding the floor of the small steps encountered throughout would also make it easier for the staff to do their jobs. Other decisions about the basement were dictated by the first floor rooms. Load-bearing walls determined where basement room locations could be. Practical reasons about use led to other decisions. It only made sense, for example, that the Kitchen remain on the back of the house beneath the formal Dining Room. Likewise, the security office was best suited close to the front entrance with access to the upper floors. A new ladies' room was planned where the old men's room had been beneath the north staircase to the basement, easy to reach by guests at functions on the first floor. A new men's room was also located close to that staircase.

Building a New Floor

Removing the existing basement rooms was not as easy as just clearing them out and starting over. First, the presence of hazardous materials such as asbestos and lead paint gave us special demolitions

Many areas of the house contained hazardous materials and had to be appropriately covered to maintain safety during the project. Courtesy DHR

headaches. Workmen had to wear appropriate masks and coveralls for protection, and authorized disposal methods for removed materials had to be followed. All suspect materials were taken away to a hazardous materials waste site.

Second, a methodical excavation and underpinning process had to be completed on the front of the house because of the damage to the foundation walls. To avoid bracing the entire foundation, a more efficient process was devised in which the walls were divided into 3.5-foot-wide sections labeled as ones, twos, or threes. Then each of the sections labeled as ones was dug out and filled with about five wheelbarrows of concrete. This "cast in place" method of underpinning was then used for all of the number two sections, and, finally, all of the threes. This process kept the load of the house distributed on the sections not being worked on and prevented extensive bracing of the entire wall.

Finally, because we believed we would find historic structures as we proceeded, we paid constant attention to what was being uncovered. The Department of Historic Resources (DHR) was a particularly important team member during the work on this floor. Their use of Sadler and Whitehead, Architects, to photograph, video and explain each day's finds created an in depth record of everything that we found. My discussion here is by no mean exhaustive of the information that they recorded, but I hope that it provides a useful starting point for anyone interested in further study.

Because of the extensive removal of modern walls, concrete floors, and altered window and door frames, the basement turned out to be a treasure trove of historic finds that showed generations of change. Work in the front rooms on the west side of the basement brought some of our first finds, especially in the EPU offices. Early doorways were revealed, one with its south jamb signed "Henry J (?)" (Jr? or Jones?) and another with its original whitewashed masonry opening found at the entrance to EPU chief Ron Watkins' office. Its large wooden header was still in place.

Behind the headers of the office windows, a system of arched wood lintels, about six inches wide and six inches high at their centers, was found appearing to support a few inches of brick along the west wall. These lintels also helped support three short floor joists for the flooring beneath the recessed windows of the Old Governor's Office above. On the outside of these basement windows, another set of wood lintels supported the brick wall. The wood of the south lintel had been replaced with steel, a modern change showing repair work had been done at some time to this window.

During the excavation to underpin the decayed foundation wall, the northwest corner of the basement showed that the original foundation walls were deeper than the other walls by more than one foot and, apparently, had always been finished at a lower depth. This was a surprise which Rob Bliley, one of the site managers for Daniel and Company, first noticed and brought it to everyone's attention. Speculation about why this was the case included the need for extra stability on that corner or perhaps a difference in the quality of the soil in that location. Whatever the reason, this new depth eliminated the need for the underpinning process in that area.

The most personal discovery in this area, however, was the message left by some of the early electricians for the house. When the EPU office ceiling was removed, a note was found that appeared penciled in haste on a scrap of packaging by those who had just finished their wiring tasks. It said, "Please look. Oct. 30, 1914. This place was wired by Martin Myers, 506 E. Main St., Richmond, Va. Work done by others: Holmes, Dutch Bottoms, John Osborne." (see picture page 45) This surely would have been some of the first electrical wiring in the building and the personal nature of the record made the discovery all the more significant. As with all of our finds, Cara Metz was notified at DHR so that proper care could be taken of this relic of past days.

There were other finds in the rooms along the front of the house. In the ceiling of the coat room, outside the Director's door, was a small opening, covered with parquet above. It may have been a vent to allow heat to rise to the Entry Hall because also in this area was a masonry pit which was probably a 20th century furnace pit or furnace room. Material that the workers described as "like what comes from a volcano" was judged by Cara Metz to be slag, the byproduct of coal burning.

Most fascinating to me were the glimpses we had of the exterior of the original Parris house, before the Duncan Lee addition, that were uncovered as the rest of the basement was excavated. These discoveries reminded us that the area of the modern kitchen did not exist in the Parris designed house and how small the original basement would have been. When the west Kitchen walls were removed, part of the original east exterior of the house with its whitewashed, Flemish bond brickwork was exposed. Removal of the small elevator, added on the original southeast exterior wall, showed more evidence of the rear side of the house.

Under the north Ballroom, when the ladies' room and surrounding spaces were removed, we made discoveries about both the first floor fireplaces and the use of the basement. Chimney bases for the Ballroom fireplaces showed that they were first built in two, arch-like piers which were later filled in the center to get a flat wall. They had double-tenon details for the hearth supports like the one found in the Director's office on the front of the house. This method of construction indicated that the fireplaces in these two areas were probably contemporaneous features.

In this same area under the north Ballroom, we found possible evidence of the place where Governor "Extra Billy" Smith moved the dining room from the first floor to the basement. Just south of the basement window on the east wall, behind hand-split lath and furring strips was an earlier finished plaster surface applied directly to the brick wall. Remnants of wallpaper adhered to the plaster and appeared to be early 19th

Wheelbarrows of cement were required to underpin the foundation of the house when it was discovered to be eroded on two sides.
Courtesy DHR

Large pieces of wallpaper were found behind lathing in the northeast basement. Dated to the 1840's it was reproduced and placed in the Lafayette Bedroom.
Courtesy DHR

century, suggesting that this space had once been used as one room. As work continued, more remnants were found delineating a room on the northeast corner. DHR was called immediately and steps were taken to preserve these features and save pieces of the wallpaper for study. Colonial Williamsburg dated a sample of the paper to the period of 1840 to 1850, exactly the time that Governor "Extra Billy" Smith was making changes to the dining arrangement of the house. In addition, no other evidence of space large enough or finished appropriately, was found that would have accommodated the basement dining room furnishings shown in a December 1848 inventory. Not only did DHR preserve samples of this wallpaper, but we decided to have it reproduced and used as the wallpaper for one of the historic rooms, the Lafayette Bedroom.

As demolition of the modern kitchen continued, more information surfaced about the eras of both Parris and Lee. The floor framing beneath the Duncan Lee Dining Room mantel was quite different from the earlier Parris mantel supports we found in the front rooms. No longer were the double-tenon joints used that we had seen beneath the first fireplaces. Now there were three headers that supported the Lee mantel, proof of their later date of installation. Evidence of the 1920s removal of the detailed structure of the Duncan Lee hearth was seen next to the east wall. The base of the fireplace was similar to that found for the front fireplaces with a double pier base. In the Kitchen, as in those beneath the Ballroom, the area between these piers was filled at some later time to create a flat wall space.

In the Kitchen service area workmen uncovered a 3'x 8' former opening in the floor framing next to the north dumbwaiter. It was oriented with its length north to south like the staircases in the front of the house, and it may have been an opening for a staircase to the 1906 Dining Room.

Despite all that we found, as with the first floor, questions still remain about the evolution of the basement and its usage. This is particularly true regarding the possible introduction to this floor of a bathroom with a shower and indoor privy. No evidence was found to secure an absolute location for these facilities, but with the Dining Room located on the northeast corner and the furnace area in the center west wall, it seems most likely if it was on this level, it was on one of the two west corners.

A New Floor Emerges

After fully photographing, video recording, and documenting the finds of the basement demolition, we were ready to begin building a new, reorganized working floor. Along the front of the house the rooms remained basically the same. With its floor lowered now, the EPU office was more comfortable for the troopers who spend many hours in this space. The office now included state of the art technology for surveillance of the house and grounds. There was still a second suite of offices beneath the Ladies' Parlor, now including a storage closet. In what we continued to use as the Director's office, the original doorway that we found was used to create a bookshelf.

Trooper Steve Canada sits in the low-ceilinged EPU office. Technology access was minimal.

Courtesy DHR

Beneath the north staircase stretching along the outside wall towards the north Ballroom is the new ladies' room, with multiple sinks and stalls. At the foot of this staircase is a new men's room, also with multiple facilities. During parties these two rooms would help alleviate the burden on the single bathroom on the first floor. They now occupy much of the area beneath the north Ballroom.

A central corridor still runs from the front offices to the Kitchen. On the north side are cabinets for storage and on the south side of the corridor is a copier and fax room used by every office in the house. Next to that on the south side is the Laundry with new machines. There is a work table there for the staff to do other tasks, and a window provides more light. Beyond the laundry we installed a new wine and beverage closet.

Chef Mark Herndon (left) and sous Chef Thomas Sauers found the newly designed kitchen much more professional.
Courtesy DHR

At the end of this main corridor there are two directions one can choose to go. Straight ahead is a door into the service area of the Kitchen, which boasts an ice machine and drink station on the left and a new restaurant style dishwasher on the right. A dumbwaiter also goes from here to a small service area off of the Dining Room and Breakfast Room. A new staircase goes up from the service area to the first floor as well.

If one goes left from the end of the main corridor, there is a hall that has additional entrances to the restrooms. Around a corner to the right is the entrance to the new building addition with a vestibule and the new elevator. Past the elevator lays the new accessible entrance for the house. A new driveway comes directly to this entrance, and people can be driven directly to the door for greater ease of entry.

The Kitchen is still on the east end of the house beneath the Dining Room. It now features a catering Kitchen that makes it more efficient for preparing food for large functions. Also it makes it easier to adhere to basic sanitation standards. The stove and oven were converted to gas, making controlling temperatures easier. Worktop areas are stainless steel. A series of sinks allows the use of appropriate methods for sanitizing cookware.

A dual walk-in refrigerator and freezer is beyond the sinks. Inside the door is the refrigerator, its walls lined with racks. The storage units make it possible to hold trays of prepared food until needed for cooking or service. Inside the refrigerator at the back is the door to the walk-in freezer.

At the north end of the Kitchen a door opens to the new addition, which provides a place for a pantry for dry and canned food storage. The new entrance, drive, and elevator to the upper floors can be reached through the pantry, making the delivery and storage of groceries convenient. Staff can move food and supplies easily to the family's kitchen on the second floor via the new elevator in the adjacent room.

This contemporary basement floor arrangement was the product of a great deal of effort and planning by many of the very people who would use it the most. Our goal had been to make the working quarters of the house well-organized, easily accessible, and safe. With the staff's valuable input, our committee was satisfied that we were successful.

An early 20th century photograph shows the northeast side of the House. The 1999 addition to give handicap access would be constructed on this corner and would balance the southeast corner which had been altered in 1958.

Courtesy Valentine Richmond History Center

CHAPTER 12

The Governor's House Welcomes Everyone

One of the greatest achievements of the entire project was placing a new wing on the northeast corner of the building. This new addition filled many needs: it restored the lost symmetry of the building; it gave much needed living and storage space; and most important, it afforded a way to provide handicap accessibility to the house without altering historic building fabric.

When first built, the Governor's House was symmetrical, actually quite plain in its original design with no side porticos or exterior embellishments at all. Gradually, from its first construction period, changes were made–north and south porticos, balustrades, a parapet, panels between the window courses were added–but all maintained an appropriate visual balance. Though the rear of the house is not one typically seen by visitors, even the Duncan Lee Dining Room addition of 1906 kept this

The north portico was added when the house was first built.

Courtesy DHR

symmetry. It wasn't until the 1930s that there began to be a loss of that regularity in the building. Governor Price, who did not like to eat in the large Lee Dining Room, had a porch built on the southeast corner. It was entered through doors added at the south end of the Dining Room. Though the porch seemed a small change on a little noticed corner, it was the first of bigger changes to come, and it was not totally without impact, as it covered the remaining east window in the south Ballroom. Still only one story, Governor Tuck had the porch made more permanent in the 1940's and finally in 1958, the Almonds had the downstairs breakfast area enlarged and added a second floor library. The library was entered through new doors from the living quarters on the second floor. The rear of the house now had noticeable asymmetry, though again, it was on the least seen corner of the building. The loss of its balanced appearance did not justify the costs related to building a matching wing in 1958. At that time, the small service road that gave motor access to the Kitchen and allowed for parking on the south side of the grounds outside the Carriage House, was already in place. The cost of relocating this road, as well as the probable condition of the ground, was prohibitive.

These same roadblocks to building the extra wing were still considerations in 1998 when we began to explore ways to make the house handicap accessible. But our commitment to making the entire house accessible was a new compelling reason to find a way to overcome the stumbling block. Our team was absolutely committed to providing access to all people who wanted to visit the Governor's House. This did not mean just the first floor, but all floors. To be sure I was aware of the difficulty that wheelchair bound guests had when they came for a tour or for receptions on the first floor; they either used a small, outdoor lift that had no cover so they were in the rain on a bad day, or they were lifted by hand up the steep front steps. When installed in the 1990s the outdoor lift had been a good initial step toward giving first floor access without changing the historic front of the building, but I was made painfully aware of how little real access that even this elevator gave to the entire residence.

Over the years the elevator had been attacked by the elements–rain, snow, piling leaves. It worked slowly and inefficiently, and to my horror one day, not at all. A young person who had been in an accident and was still a patient at nearby Medical College of Virginia, was still confined to a wheelchair. His parents wanted a place to take him on his first outing from the hospital, and we offered the Governor's House since it was near the hospital and would be not crowded. It did not occur to us that there would be any difficulty getting him in, and as he always did, Tutti made certain the elevator and the house were ready. I walked out with Tutti and we greeted the family. The nurse wheeled the chair onto the lift. The lift creaked as it started upward and then suddenly it stopped, refusing to go either up or down, suspended halfway in the confining cubicle of the shaft. Our young guest was frightened, as were we all

A lift from ground level to the level of the first floor was exposed to the weather. Those using it would get wet in the rain. The lift frequently stuck, stranding its occupant.

Courtesy DHR

since nothing that we did brought the lift back to life. It seemed like an eternity until Tutti finally pressed the button and it lurched upward. But my awakening to the shortcomings of the access to the House didn't stop then, for as we entered the house I realized that there was no way for our guest to go up to the second floor to our sons' rooms. He couldn't go down to the basement to see the troopers space or see the Kitchen. The inside elevator was too small and the double course of steps quite high and steep to carry someone up or down in a wheelchair. This was one of those moments that I realized that what we were planning was absolutely the right thing to do, and that we had to find a way to blend necessity and history.

We began to examine and reject proposals for meeting our new demands. One dismissed plan put forward the idea of making the location of the existing elevator, in the center of the building in the arch between the Ballroom and Dining Room, larger and capable of housing the size elevator needed. This plan came up short for several reasons. First, this location did not even address the need of providing a covered entrance into the house for those in wheelchairs. Second, to provide the space necessary for the larger elevator we would have to have removed the arch where the current elevator was housed. This would have destroyed the connection that Duncan Lee had made with his changes to the original form of Alexander Parris in the front of the house. Finally, we weren't just trying to add a new elevator, but we were also trying to accommodate accessible bathrooms. When we arrived, there was not one accessible restroom in the entire house. Keeping the elevator where it was gave us nothing toward solving any of these issues.

By August 1998 it had become clear that the desire to make the Governor's House ADA compliant was going to dictate many of the project's choices and that these choices had to be made early in order to stay on schedule. In a project charrette held on August 5, 1998, John Paul Hanbury put forth the recommendation for an addition on the northeast rear corner of the Governor's House that would mirror the addition that was made on the southeast corner of the House in the 1950s; he opined that this was the best way to make the House accessible and not completely destroy the historic first floor. This addition would give the House a new accessible entrance, space for an accessible elevator to all floors, and an accessible bathroom on the first floor. Moreover it would give extra storage space for the Kitchen in the basement and for the first time a full kitchen in the living quarters on the second floor. The addition had the added architectural benefit of restoring symmetry to the exterior of the building. While these gains of the addition were significant, they would not be without a huge impact on the Governor's House grounds.

At the end of the south side of the house, an old hackberry tree hung ominously over the house. Its limbs were wired to the trunk to keep them from falling on the house. Courtesy DHR

The Governor's House Welcomes Everyone

A new gate into the west wall provides access to the Carriage House and rear parking area. Courtesy DHR

The first problem was that the addition would be in the path of the small access driveway around the rear of the House to the Carriage House. This drive would either have to be moved or eliminated in order to accommodate the new structure. Several options were studied. Initial cost projections found that relocating the road lower on the bank along Governor Street would be prohibitive. In the alternate plan which was eventually adopted, the original drive would be stopped at the entrance of the addition. A new walkway bordered by a formal garden would be constructed along the top of the hill along the rear of the House. The drive would provide access to the new entrance, especially to the Kitchen, and the walkway would allow for new landscaping along the hill. But the loss of the old road meant that there was no vehicle access to the Carriage House. A new entrance would have to be constructed for the Carriage House and parking area. We developed a plan for a new drive to enter the complex along the southwest wall of the grounds by the corner of the Old Finance Building (now the Oliver Hill Building). The plan called for the construction of a gate into the existing brick wall. This new West Gate proposal was examined carefully since the hill of Capitol Square begins to drop off dramatically down to Governor Street. The drive could not be too steep for cars and trucks to maneuver.

Once the plans for the addition were adopted and the decision was made to proceed with eliminating the service road and adding the West Gate, we officially expanded the scope of the project to include renovations of both the Carriage House and Cottage and sought additional funding from the General Assembly for these two buildings. The original appropriation for the Governor's House alone was $4.985M. Though the cost of the addition would be at least partially offset by eliminating costs for changes that would no longer have to be made in the original structure, the addition of the two buildings, the new gate, and the drive into the compound expanded the project and would require an increase of the appropriation. The final amount spent on the entire project was $7.285M.

The expansion in scope had impacts on the project other than funding. The large increase in construction would have an effect on the site. Trev Crider from DGS informed the team that a new environmental impact statement would be required, and Bill Crosby from Historic Resources said that an archaeologist would need to assess any historic features that might be uncovered in excavating the foundation for the new addition or West Gate.

While the West Gate excavation yielded artifacts that were possibly associated with an early smokehouse (see Chapter 1), the area of the new foundation was not as fruitful. The soil there seemed to be mostly fill, and no artifacts were discovered. However, as the excavation for the new elevator shaft was started, the stepped brick footing of the north wall of the 1906 addition was exposed.

Gains of the New Addition

The gains of the new addition were numerous and brought solutions to many long existing problems. Wheelchair entry through the new side door was easy. Vehicles could park right at the doorway for close access and limited exposure to the elements for those in wheelchairs. Once inside, the elevator, with its door faux-finished and resembling paneling, was in the hallway to the right. There were restrooms just beyond the elevator. To the left of the new main entrance was a door to a new pantry and dry goods storage room for the Kitchen. This entry made the delivery of Kitchen needs convenient.

The elevator went from the basement hall to vestibules on the first and second floors. On the first floor one stepped into a hall where a door on the right immediately opened into the north Ballroom. This door was where one of the Ballroom windows had been (see Chapter 8). Decorating the hall on the left side of the Ballroom door was the case for the Steuben glass bowl that had originally been in the north hallway outside the small restroom. For the walls here we chose a wonderful paper by Scalamandre, Lyre, with a pale yellow background and blue and gold ribbons and leaves which echoed those from the Chloe paper in the adjacent Ballroom.

Directly across from the elevator was a hidden door that entered a butler's pantry off of the Dining Room. This door was installed to facilitate bringing food service needs from the basement to the Dining Room. The remainder of the addition on the first floor was a new accessible powder room. Through a door on the left as one exited the elevator, the room had large windows that made the space bright and airy. There was adequate room for two separate areas for the toilet and sinks. We continued using Lyre in the powder room, and to take advantage of the natural light from the windows, we trimmed the curtains in a cadet blue fabric with a white and crystal trim by Scalamandre.

On the second floor, the elevator opened between the family room on the right and a new family kitchen on the left. One of the major drawbacks of the Governor's House for a family had always been its lack of a true kitchen anywhere but in the basement. Now there was room for the family to have a state of the art kitchen with space to put a table and four chairs for dining.

It is hard to pick the parts of the restoration project that were the most important, but the team's decision to go forward with the northeast wing is certainly among them. The addition addressed two of the aspects of the work that were most important to me–making the house comfortable and accessible for all, and preserving as many of its historic elements as we could. I hope that it has given more people the opportunity to visit their Governor's Home and learn about its history and the people who have lived there.

The renovated Charles Gillette Garden is a tribute to the efforts of the Garden Club of Virginia to preserve historic gardens. Using Gillette's original plans and lists of plants, William D. Rieley, ASLA, recreated Gillette's spectacular design and array of spring colors, a serene oasis from the bustle of Capitol Square. It is said that Gillette helped select the fountain statue of Daphne transforming into the laurel tree, no doubt the reason for the inclusion of laurels in the garden.

Courtesy William D. Rieley, ASLA

CHAPTER 13

Expanding the Project to the Whole Compound—
Carriage House, Cottage and The Gillette Garden

Almost all building projects at the Governor's House had expanded their scope even before the first tasks were started. From the initial construction in 1813 when it was decided that porches should be added to the Parris design before the building was ever finished, to the changes that Governor "Extra Billy" Smith made in the 1840s to accommodate his large family, construction plans at the House have burgeoned to encompass more than originally planned. Though tight management was maintained through careful planning in the 1998 restoration, nonetheless our project was no exception in its additions to scope.

Stopping the ongoing deterioration of the Governor's House and giving it modern systems were the initial goals of the restoration. The General Assembly had allocated funds for several years for these missions but they had never been used. However the scope quickly began to grow investigations into the condition of the building started to reveal the true magnitude of the task. Some decisions for project add-ons were driven by the needs of the house itself and others by the layout of the complex of buildings that stood around it.

The grounds of the Governor's House had been in a compound-like area since a brick wall was added for security purposes in 1954. Ever since that time the Governor's House complex has been separate from Capitol Square with no entry into the compound except by the guard house at the front gate. Within this walled enclosure are several buildings which are important in the day-to-day operation of activities at the House. It soon began to make sense to include these buildings in the 1998 project due to their con-

The Governor's House sits behind a circular drive within a walled complex. It is approached directly through Capitol Square from the Washington statue.
Courtesy DHR

dition which was on a par with the residence. To leave the problems of these buildings unaddressed was not prudent.

Connected to the Governor's House by a walkway that was added in the 1840s is a building known today as the Cottage. Contemporaneous with the Governor's House, this building was the first kitchen. Food had to be carried into the main House to the Dining Room which was on the first floor when the house was first built and was in later years moved to the basement. Originally a stand-alone, two-story structure, the building housed the kitchen on its first floor and servant quarters on the second floor; it had a small herb garden in the rear. In the 1920s when it was no longer needed for these functions, Governor Byrd had the rooms redone and the building began to be used as a guest house or by some administrations as rooms for their children and was called the Cottage. Still an integral part of life at the Governor's House, the Cottage borders one side of the formal garden designed by Charles Gillette in the 1950s and is connected to the main house by walkways on both the first floor and basement levels.

In 1998 the Cottage and walkways had structural and system problems like those of the Governor's House. HVAC, plumbing and wiring were all outdated. Water wicked up through the brick walls causing the interior plaster walls to blister and the paint to pop off. Ever since the administration of Governor Wilder, the walkway from the Cottage to the main house had contained a small unenclosed elevator. In an effort to make the Governor's House handicap accessible, this lift was installed alongside the walkway that would raise a wheelchair up to the level of the first floor of the House. By 1998 weather had taken its toll on this lift and its operation was undependable. However, it was the only wheelchair access to the building, and in fact the only accessible feature at the house. There were no accessible restrooms in the house and wheelchair access to any floor other than the

Tony Griffin, Director of the Capitol Grounds service, discusses the layout of the herb garden behind the Cottage.
Courtesy DHR

LEFT: *The Carriage House had office space on the end of the building and two garage bays for automobiles.*
RIGHT: *The stairs down into the Gillette Garden at the walkway from the house to the cottage needed repair.*

Courtesy DHR

first floor was virtually impossible.

Outside of the Cottage, the Gillette Garden was still a beautiful and serene retreat from the bustle of Capitol Square. But none of Gillette's original plant species were there any longer and borders and pool needed extensive maintenance.

Beyond the garden wall on the south end were two buildings that were also part of the Governor's House complex. One building was an old greenhouse that in its heyday boasted potted plants and flowers that were used throughout the House and yard. One inventory from the late 1800s shows 2000 clay pots, and inspection of photographs, especially from the early 1900s, shows clay potted palms scattered throughout the Governor's House and yard. The greenhouse was long past its prime and, like much throughout the compound, in a state of disrepair.

Also at the south end of the complex is a large building known as the Carriage House. The Carriage House is a two story building, about 85' by 16', which was originally used as stables, then a garage and office complex. When we arrived, the second floor (ground level with the Cottage and formal garden) had areas used for storage as well as a garage. The first floor had quarters where some staff occasionally stayed overnight if they were needed at early morning events. Also on the first floor were rooms that could be accessed only from the alley at the rear of the building. These rooms were used by buildings and grounds for maintenance equipment, shop and office areas.

Like the Governor's House and Cottage, the Carriage House was in dire need of attention. HVAC, electrical, and plumbing systems were all outdated. The area outside of the Carriage House was still used to park cars—governors' personal vehicles, Executive Protection vehicles, personal vehicles of staff— with the only access to this area a small drive that ran from the north side and front gate of the Governor's House along the rear of the house, almost touching the house at some places along its east side. The driveway area and hillside down to Governor Street was overgrown with shrubs and trees, with some of the limbs of an old Hackberry tree being held onto the tree by wires so they didn't fall onto the Governor's bedroom.

The condition of these structures along with their location in the Governor's House complex made it clear that their needs should not be omitted in the renovation project. Moreover, our decision to make the Governor's House handicap accessible while still maintaining the historic nature of the building was leading to changes that were going to affect access to the Carriage House and parking area whether or not the buildings were renovated.

All of these changes in scope had the potential of derailing the tight time schedule that was in place for the restoration. In order not to upset the six-month deadline placed by the Governor, work done on the Carriage House and Cottage and the new West Gate entry was begun before our family moved to temporary quarters. Actual construction on these new project pieces joined the preconstruction examination of the House to find any hidden issues that needed to be resolved, discussions with the staff to get their input on their needs and desired improvements, and the development of the plans that would be put into place inside the main house. The greenhouse was demolished and excavations for the West Gate, new power feeds, and sewer lines for the complex were begun in December, 1998.

It was during the excavation for the West Gate that a pocket of artifacts was found that gave brief hope that the foundation of the first house on the site had been found. Brickwork and artifacts were excavated and examined, and we concluded that these were likely the remnants of an old smokehouse that was shown on a map of Capitol Square, or perhaps part of the drains of an icehouse that had also been in the area. This area was treated as a salvage archaeology project and work was halted so that an appropriate study of the area could be made and recorded. Cara Metz of the Department of Historic Resources headed this excavation. Though Cara was also involved in the excavation at the site of the new addition, there were no artifacts found in that area.

The Carriage House

The Carriage House emerged from the renovation a new complex of office space, temporary staff accommodations, and storage and work space for the grounds crews. Its second floor (on the same level as the Cottage and formal garden) had three rooms on the east end of the building which could be used as offices. While I was First Lady, my assistant, Stacy Hight, had her office in the end room overlooking Governor Street. Separated from her office by a hall was a second room used for copying, faxing, and work space; this area had a small restroom as well. The third room was set aside for storage and use by volunteers who came to address or stuff envelopes for official Governor's House functions. There is a stairway down to the first floor from this third office space. Adjacent to these three offices is a double bay garage. Next to these bays I set up my office in a fourth large room which also has a small restroom. It is opposite the gate into the garden. This space is quiet, away from the bustle of the main house, and despite being separated by the garage bays from the other offices, was still close enough to make working there very convenient.

On the first floor of the Carriage House are rooms that can be used in different ways, depending on the needs of the current administration. For our use, the rooms on the east end of the first floor, including a bathroom with a shower, were for security and staff. There was a lounge where the stairs came down from the second floor which could be used by staff for various needs and by those working at House functions when they were not needed inside. Adjacent to these rooms and beneath the garage bays was the mechanical room which can be accessed only from the rear alley. Next to the mechanical room is another room with access only from the alley that was used as an office by Tony Griffin, the Director of Capital Grouds Service. A final room on the west end of the first floor provided storage space and had a staircase up to the second floor/ground level. As with all work done during the renovation, flexibility of space was always important, and future administrations could use and decorate this non-historic space according to their own needs.

The Cottage

The Cottage is contemporaneous with the Governor's House and thus one of the oldest buildings in Capitol Square. It was first built as a stand-alone kitchen. Its first floor had two rooms with a hall and stairway bisecting the building and separating the rooms. The second floor copied that configuration with two rooms and a hall. Each of the four rooms had a fireplace, with large hearths in the first floor rooms. When it was no longer used as the kitchen, bathrooms were added on each floor at some unknown time; by 1998 these were dated in their construction. The bathroom on the first floor had been placed along the west side of the room closest to the main residence and formed a hallway along the rear of the downstairs. It took

The loggia outside the Cottage borders on the Gillette Garden and is a pleasant place to spend quiet time away from the bustle of Capitol Square.
Courtesy DHR

space from the original room but was necessary because a bathroom was essential to the continued use of the Cottage. The bathroom on the second floor was at the head of the stairs and was shared by the two upstairs rooms.

One of the most significant problems that the Cottage had was that the lower course of bricks wicked water through them and continuously damaged the plaster walls. Many things had been tried in the past to stop this destructive process, but none had succeeded. We installed a new drainage system on the exterior of the building to channel water away from the foundation and thus slow this process.

While the Cottage will always retain its rustic charm with its brick walls and wide board floors, during the restoration all of the mechanical systems were updated and new bathrooms installed. An accessible shower was included in the second floor bathroom. Because the Cottage had primarily been used as bedrooms, either for guests or children, we treated most of the rooms this way. The large room on the first floor, however, was kept as a recreation room with television, movie access, and comfortable furniture. It was a nice room to have while entertaining in the garden in case people wanted to come indoors for some reason. Our son, Ashton, was even able to keep his ping pong table there, which could be closed and moved out of the way if necessary.

After the water wicking had been addressed and new plaster installed, the walls of the large room were covered with the teal on putty version of the Brunschwig and Fils wallpaper Fox and Rooster. The other room on the first floor was kept as a bedroom, with the window treatment and bed skirts in another Brunschwig and Fils pattern, a Grilly cotton print in cream. Its walls were whitewashed plaster and some kitchen elements were left in the fireplace, reminiscent of its original use. After the attacks of 9-11 (September 11, 2001), when security was maintained at the house around the clock, some EPU members would use that room for overnight accommodations.

Both rooms on the second floor were treated as bedrooms which we used for visiting family members and guests. The fabrics in the north room were cream and charcoal toiles from the Mount Vernon Collection of Brunschwig and Fils, and this theme was carried into the bathroom as well. Guests that used the Cottage said that it gave them the wonderful experience of being at the Governor's House, access to the House by the walkway, but at the same time privacy in their own, historic space overlooking the garden.

The Charles Gillette Garden

There is no name more synonymous with landscape architecture in Richmond, than Charles Gillette. Gillette designed many of the premier gardens of both private homes and public spaces such as the Governor's House. Gillette was engaged to design and install a formal, walled garden on the south side of the house. From 1954 to 1956 he worked to create a colorful, serene refuge from the bustle of the mid-city rush that could be entered from a walkway from the south hall of the first floor. The Cottage borders the garden on the west side and can be entered through the veranda ground level from the garden. The walkway from the house forms the veranda below and creates a balcony for the cottage that overlooks the garden, with entrances onto the balcony from each of the second floor bedrooms of the Cottage.

Over the years the walled border of the garden retained the Gillette layout, but only a single bush remained of the original vegetation. Fortunately, Gillette's detailed drawings of the garden and lists of plants

The Gillette Garden required extensive ground work and brick work to return it to its original Gillette design. The Garden Club of Virginia assumed the task of the garden restoration.
Courtesy DHR

and their locations remained. With the scope of the Governor's House renovation already at capacity, the Restoration Committee asked the Garden Club of Virginia through its Restoration Committee to take on the task of restoring the garden for the Commonwealth. The Garden Club is known for the quality of their projects as well as their desire that projects that they undertake be maintained in meticulous detail. Numerous meetings were held between Secretary of Administration Bryan Slater, President of the Garden Club of Virginia, Nancy St. Clair Talley (Mrs. Lilburn T. Talley), Landscape Architect for the Garden Club of Virginia, William D. Rieley, ASLA, and me to discuss the guidelines of the project and the Commonwealth's willingness to keep the garden as restored. The Garden Club voted in October 1999 to proceed with the restoration, and work was begun right away so that the major plantings could be in place and ready for visitors by April 2000. Rieley admitted that he was quite nervous as a wet winter hindered progress. Plantings were being installed right up to the end, but on a glorious spring day we were able to proudly open the garden and express our sincere appreciation for the Garden Club of Virginia.

The New Guard House

Since 1954, entry to the Governor's House grounds was through a gate in the brick wall that surrounds the grounds. It is reported that in 1961 Josephine Almond worried about the guards having to stand watch in the elements and insisted that a small, telephone booth structure be added for their convenience. In

1961, despite the objections of the historical review committee for Capitol Square which objected to a structure at the gate, the telephone booth was converted to a permanent brick building. While it was a great improvement over standing outside, even this enclosure had limited heat in the winter and no air conditioning, and little in the way of security other than a telephone.

One of the major areas we studied for upgrades during the restoration was the security system in place for the Governor's House, and the guard house fell into this examination. Adding to the issue of its sparse accommodations for the guards, the current structure could not house the needs of the new system of security that was being proposed. We decided to build a new facility that would not only give more adequate security, but would provide more space for those on duty at the gate.

While it might seem that building a new guard house would be an easy task, it involved more than just enlarging the size of the room. A new guard house would have to be big enough to accommodate the new electronic security system and HVAC improvements but appropriately placed and not so large as to detract from the view of the Governor's House. As seen in 19th century photographs on page 20, when the House was first built, the grounds were open, with only an iron fence surrounding the yard. It remained this way for years, and access was limited to the house only by the 1954 brick wall. The wall had already lessened the view of the Governor's House from Capitol Square and a bigger guard house could have even more of an impact on the view of the House. Not wanting to detract further from the view, John Paul Hanbury constructed a full sized façade of the proposed guard house that he placed at different spots along the wall in order to actually see what it would look like in different locations.

The new Guard House stands at the north side of the Main Gate into the Governor's House complex. It is larger than the small house had been, with room for more than one officer, and it has more electronic surveillance equipment that ties into the security system for the House and Capitol Square.

FROM LEFT: *John Paul Hanbury, John Mitchell, Sam Daniel, Bryan Slater and Donald Williams prepare to examine a mockup of a new guard house.*   Courtesy DHR

Though our restoration project was like many others before, expanding from its very beginning, the benefits that were gained by the enlargement were worth the additional resources. We were able to make the house fully accessible to all people for the first time. We saved two additional buildings that were rapidly deteriorating and made them the beneficial resources they should have been. Today the entire Governor's House complex is a secure, comfortable setting for family, staff and guests. What will it need in another 100 years?

Postscript

By Christmas we were back, finally unpacked and ready to spend the remaining two years of Jim's term in the Governor's House. I didn't realize it at the time, but we had really been like Governor James Barbour, living in a neighboring Richmond dwelling and watching as the house was constructed. But unlike Governor Barbour who just saw the house at its beginning, we had seen the evolution of the house from the days of Alexander Parris, to the sweeping changes of Duncan Lee, to glimpses of the basement Dining Room of Governor "Extra Billy" Smith. We had seen the traces left by workmen of the past. To the modern additions of a Breakfast Room and library, we had added accessibility to the house so that all could visit and live comfortably.

As I reflect on the life of this place, and the lives of those who had been there before us, I realize now that as long as new families arrive every four years, this house will go on evolving, especially in the family quarters and working areas of the basement. We tried to create a comfortable place for them to build on and enjoy.

But I hope as well, with the 200th anniversary of the Governor's House on the horizon, that making history be the top priority on the first floor will continue. Like so many of Virginia's treasured homes of the past, the Governor's House has stories to tell. And I know from talking to all of the visitors who came to tour and to people when I traveled across the state, the people of Virginia love their history and want to preserve it.

By Christmas 1999 Jim, Jay, Ashton and I had moved back into the House and were ready for Christmas. We used this Christmas card to invite Virginians to visit their newly restored Governor's House on New Year's Day, 2000.

Author's Collection

APPENDIX

The Hands that Made it Happen

The restoration of a historic building requires the expertise of a variety of artisans to work on the fundamental structural elements that make old buildings special. Saving these elements makes each project not only unique, but also a challenge. In modern structures many of the old methods of building have been replaced by new elements and new methods of construction. Finding craftsmen who still work in the old techniques can be difficult. Sheetrock has replaced plaster work; pre-formed or machine cut wood pieces have replaced hand carved wood decorations, and ready-made curtains have replaced hand cut and styled window treatments. The numbers of people who still perform these types of hand work are becoming fewer with time.

Assembling the variety of craftsmen that were needed for the Governor's House was a top priority of the project coordinators because we believed that only quality workmanship would ensure making the restoration a success. Every aspect of the house needed experts: the structural elements, the furnishings, and the grounds. Often the workmen who were needed were the only individuals still at work in their field and there was no way to get bids other than theirs. This was in opposition to the Commonwealth's bid requirements, and sometimes we needed special permission to use "single source" vendors. This limited pool of workers made it even more critical that the project be undertaken when it was, so that these special features of the building could be retained.

The team of artisans that we ultimately assembled was committed to maintaining or restoring as much of the original structure of the Governor's House as possible. From the outside porches to the secluded

Breakfast Room, special help was needed to complete this goal. Those who participated in this effort are to be commended for their talents and contributions. I have included some of these craftsmen and their work in the main text. Others are treated in more detail here. All were indispensable to the success of the restoration.

Custom Woodworking. The front porch that welcomes every visitor to the Governor's House has four free-standing columns and two columns that efface the building, each decorated with a Corinthian capital at its top. Over time these pieces had become damaged and the top Acanthus leaves were broken off. There was no way to just buy leaves that would match, so we made a search to find someone who could repair the column to correspond to the others. Since the first sight anyone who comes to the house has is the front porch, this is a detail that could not be overlooked. This is but one example of the detailed woodwork–door jambs, chair rails, and more– that had to be repaired. Custom millwork of this kind was done by Premier Millwork and Lumber Company of Virginia Beach. Stephen Benda, Senior Estimator, traveled frequently from Virginia Beach to oversee his firm's work. In a conversation with me he recalled "John Paul Hanbury calling periodically to say he had another piece of molding from the early 19th century that we needed to match exactly–and have it done in 24 hours!" He shares a vivid memory of mine of James S. Brockman, a carver from the Pungo area of the Beach, busily at work on the front porch capitals. In order to do his work he sat perched atop a ladder, refining his hand-carved replacement pieces.

The parquet floor conservation required yet another set of skills brought to the project by Fred Ecker II of Tidewater Preservation, Inc. of Fredericksburg. Many of the floor pieces were damaged beyond repair, the floor squeaked beyond the limits of being acceptably nostalgic, and the floor's finish was scratched, scraped and faded. The easiest route was perhaps to replace the floor altogether, to basically start over. This would mean the loss of an important historic element of the building. But Ecker's study showed that the floor could be saved. Injections were made from the basement level between the subfloor and the parquet to cushion the parquet level and quiet it. Pieces of parquet salvaged from the side hallways were specially cut to repair rotted and worn curved pieces for the oval shaped Dining Room. And the latest in floor finishing was used to try to protect the floor from its high use wear and tear. Our goal was to save a floor that was perfectly good and keep it in as good shape as possible until perhaps a new process could be developed to give it lasting life.

Faux Finishing and Marbleizing. Faux finishing is a process where basic building features are made to look like they are made from other, usually more expensive materials. Cost restraints, material availability and even current fashion can drive the use of faux-finishing. Its use dates to ancient times, and it is still a very sought after technique in today's designs. During the initial investigative stage of the renovation, we researched paint to try to determine original wall colors. Not only did we examine the walls, but also doors, columns, and column bases. This research verified that the doors were original to the house and had originally been faux-finished to look like wood-grained mahogany. When the doors were completely stripped, despite the discovery of heat damage from earlier finish removal, an even more complete picture of

Using a feather Elaine Tucker faux finished the Ballroom column bases to look like marble. Courtesy DHR

their appearance emerged showing the ghosts of box locks. Moldings and column bases were also examined during the paint research and revealed the colors and likely style of these features. Though evidence from the examination was inconclusive, it is likely that the bases of the interior columns were marbleized. Elaine Hamilton Tucker, a specialist in faux finishing, was engaged to return the mahogany appearance to the doors and marbleize the column bases.

Scalamandre. Scalamandre Silks, founded in 1929 by Franco and Flora Scalamandre, was for years a leader in the reproduction of antique textiles. Franco Scalamandre and his daughter Adrianna Scalamandre Bitter worked closely with Jacqueline Kennedy in the refurbishment of the White House during the Kennedy administration. Scalamandre Silks also produced the textile collection for Prestwould, a magnificent Virginia estate on the eastern bank of the Roanoke River. This Prestwould Collection was the result of a more than ten-year long project preserving the fabrics and wall coverings of the late 18th century plantation of Sir Peyton Skipwith. These collections were the sources of many of the fabrics and wall coverings used in the Governor's House restoration.

In the Ladies' Parlor a Prestwould gold, blue, and light red border set the palette of colors for that room. For the Ballroom the vibrant blue of the Blue Room of the White House was the inspiration. "Chloe," an elegant blue, gray and gold wallpaper border from the Scalamandre Prestwould collection, adorns the ceiling line. Following this color scheme, Barbara Page proposed window treatments like those of the White House Blue Room, echoing the changes made by Duncan Lee who was inspired in his work for these rooms by the White House. These draperies, festooned with swags and jabots, were designed and hand sewn by Ruth Hubbard and Kathryn Arnold of the Colonial Williamsburg Drapery Studio. Other fabrics and wall coverings from Scalamandre were used in the private living quarters on the second floor.

One of the most fabulous trips that I took during the renovation was to visit the Scalamandre fabric and paper mill in Long Island City, New York. Owner Mark Bitter and President Bob Bitter gave me a personal tour of their 75-year-old brick building filled with antique jacquard looms, spinning wheels and silk screens. With me on the tour were Governor's House Director Donna Case, Vernon Edenfield of The Kenmore Foundation who had introduced us to the Scalamandre team, and Barbara Page our interior designer from Hanbury-Evans.

On our tour we saw the production of wall coverings. This process began with the hand-mixing of the paints by three workers who blended the colors by "eye" to the correct shade, adding spoonsful of pigment as needed. Donna wondered what would happen to this process should anything happen to those mixing the paints, as there was no recorded formula for the shades of colors. After mixing, these paints were meticulously applied through silk screen

Scalamandre fabrics and wood mold tassels were used throughout the first floor because of their historic quality.
Courtesy DHR

patterns to a long strip of paper which was unrolled onto long wooden table-like forms. The colors were added one at a time to the paper and allowed to dry before another color was applied. The completed paper then was rolled into the familiar rolls that we know as wallpaper.

The tour continued on another floor where women seated in a circle were hand-making drapery tassels by winding fine silk thread around the variously shaped wooden molds that form the base of each tassel. Imagine trying to wind, by hand, the thinnest thread possible, as flat and evenly as you can, onto an old-fashioned wooden spool–but instead of a spool it is a ball or teardrop shaped wooden form. It is a task that takes true skill and extraordinary patience. We used our tassels to adorn drapery edges and ribbons sewn along drapery, swags and jabots.

We also toured the workshop where silk fabrics were being upholstered onto furniture. While in this workshop, I saw a sofa being upholstered with Hillwood, a grotto blue custom fabric reproduced from the estate of Marjorie Merriweather Post. I thought the design and color of the fabric were perfect for the new Ballroom color we had chosen, and Barbara Page worked to have this fabric included on the two Duncan Fife sofas in the Ballroom, which had been gifts of Mr. and Mrs. George Kaufman of Norfolk.

Colonial Williamsburg Drapery Studio. When the decision was made to use Scalamandre fabrics as the core of the new furnishings, it was imperative to find experts who could produce the complex design of the draperies needed and take the necessary care with the delicate fabrics. Ruth Hubbard and Kathryn Arnold from the Design Studio at Colonial Williamsburg were perfect for the task. Working closely together with Barbara Page, Ruth and her team skillfully created window treatments appropriate to each room of the Governor's House.

I traveled to Williamsburg one afternoon and visited the design shop. In a small, almost cramped space in the Kingsmill area of Williamsburg I found the ladies working on the draperies for the Old Governor's Office. Not wanting to pin and cut the Scalamandre fabrics without a trial run, Ruth had collected old bed sheets to "practice on," using these patterns she had cut from Barbara's designs for the better fabrics. Her practice included hanging the pieces to see how they draped and to check their proportions. After the patterns were made and tested in the design shop, the drapery team traveled to Richmond and tested each pattern at a window in the house to make certain that the proportions were correct for the window and the room. There was nothing left to chance in the planning phase of the draperies because of the delicacy and value of the fabrics that would adorn the windows. Only after this long planning process did Ruth cut the actual fabrics and hand-sew them together.

Ruth Hubbard of the Colonial Williamsburg Drapery Studio went to extra lengths to practice on sheets and get the designs perfect before cutting the expensive drapery fabrics.

One of the most amazing things I encountered on moving to Capitol Square was the collection of poorly stored "cast off" draperies and furnishings from the Governor's House. The Old State Finance Building, now called the Oliver Hill Building, housed racks of draperies in a dark, damp basement area with little climate control; previous administrations had decided these draperies were no longer useful in the house. There were assorted dishes and glassware stacked there as well. Our team hoped that this type of castoff collection would be avoided in the future with the historic research that we put into design and the quality of the fabrics and workmanship in the project; furnishings of the quality selected during the renovation should last for years with proper care.

Ruth Hubbard and her team were particularly attentive to our desire to conserve still useful elements of the existing house. Ruth determined that there was ample fabric in the current Ballroom draperies to serve as linings for the Old Governor's Office and Ladies' Parlor windows, thus preventing throwing away quality fabric.

In addition to their work on the first floor of the house, the drapery team also created a bedroom ensemble for the historic Lafayette Bedroom. Barbara Page selected George Washington's bedroom at Mount Vernon as a model for the window treatments and bed hangings that Ruth and her production team followed and created. The fabric for the window and bed hangings was a Brunschwig and Fils white New Richmond Dimity that was dramatically set off by the custom made wall covering and border made by Carter and Company.

After the draperies had all been completed, Ruth approached me about creating a special collection of handmade angels to be clad in robes made from otherwise unusable remnants of the Scalamandre drapery material. Based on the angel tree that is the Christmas hallmark at the Metropolitan Museum of Art in New York City, these angels would adorn the Governor's House Christmas Tree. The angels were of varying size and pose, and the rich colors of the fabrics made for spectacular presentation on the tree. The first Christmas that we were back in the house after the renovation, we placed the Christmas tree, adorned by the angels, in the center of the Ballroom. The second Christmas after completion of the renovation, I decided to dedicate the tree to all of the historic homes of Virginia. I had each angel on the tree "hold" a Christmas ornament from a historic site in Virginia. The small ornaments that were used had been gifts to me for my efforts in promoting historic preservation and tourism to benefit the historic places of Virginia. At an annual meeting of the Virginia Tourism Corporation each historic home of Virginia gave me a Christmas ornament from their site. These were the ornaments that were used on the angel tree

Our first Christmas Tree after the restoration was filled with angels handmade by Ruth Hubbard from remnants of fabrics used in the first floor rooms. Courtesy DHR

that year, and I still have a tree each Christmas in my home with only those brass ornaments.

Woodward Grosvenor and Company, Ltd., Kiddeminster, England. While teaching a study abroad course for Randolph-Macon College, I had the opportunity to visit the Woodward Grosvenor and Company, Ltd. which is housed in the historic Stourvale Mill in Kiddeminster, England. The company's Stourvale Mill Collection is one of the largest collections of archival point papers for carpets, including over 10,000 patterns. In this collection, Barbara Page and John Paul Hanbury had found the antique Brussels rug patterns that were period appropriate for our historic rooms and presented their choices to me. For the Old Governor's Office and Ladies' Parlor there was an 1810 pattern that would be loomed in the same manner as original Brussels style carpets. Another Federal style pattern was chosen for the Entry Hall.

When I learned that I would be near the mill during my trip, I made arrangements for a Randolph-Macon colleague, Greg Daugherty, and me to visit it, see the original point papers of the patterns, and watch a similar rug being loomed. On this trip I learned how pattern is set by the cards and the yarn colors are loaded onto the loom according to the cards, carried along the back of the carpet and drawn up to the surface also according to the pattern cards.

The pile of these Brussels carpets is not cut and creates a durable, level loop finish that makes them more practical than cut pile carpets such as Wilton. Wilton carpets were used by only the wealthiest families because of their expense, about twice that of Brussels style. The less costly, more durable Brussels carpets were saved for the heavy use areas of the house. There is evidence in saved receipts that there were Brussels carpets in the Governor's House, though no pattern information was saved. It seems from its earliest days the Commonwealth was making cost saving choices, including putting serviceable carpets in the Governor's House.

Brussels carpets were produced in 27-inch widths and shipped in bales on ships. When they arrived a purchaser could select whatever was available in the bales. The strips would be delivered to the home where they were hand sewn together for a complete carpet. This is still the way that these carpets are created. Though our carpets were ordered through J. R. Burroughs and Company in Rockland, Massachusetts and we didn't have to go down to the dock to pick out our pattern from those in the shipped bales, when our 27-inch widths of new carpet arrived at the house, it took days of matching patterns and sewing to install the pieces wall-to-wall in the two parlors. The hall rug also had to be joined, but it was loose laid and bound like an oriental rug to make a transition from the 1813 area of the house to the Classical Revival style of the adjoining Ballroom. The installation of our carpets was done by Peter Mead of Four Quarter Carpets in Orange.

One of the major concerns I had about the color scheme that had been chosen for the Governor's House was allayed when I visited the Stourvale mill. The new colors of the house were going to follow the historic paint research that had been done and a dramatic new color palette had emerged–muted gray and taupe on the walls and carpets to be accented by rose, burgundy, gold, and blue in the fabrics. This would be a striking change from the light yellow and bold pink that had dominated the house in the past and perhaps questioned despite its historic validation. But at Stourvale I found that the original colors penciled on the backs of the point papers for the carpets were "gray," "drab," "dark drab," and "light drab." These muted colors were fashionable in the early 1800s for basic areas and then accented by much bolder colors in wall coverings and fabrics. The color choice that had been made was exactly right for the period and the carpets being used.

Moreover, in the center of the pattern that would go in both the Old Governor's Office and the Ladies' Parlor there was a spider-web image that was reflective of the plaster decorations in the ceilings of both rooms.

Portrait of Queen Elizabeth. The oldest and among the most valuable pieces in the Governor's House at the time of the renovation was a portrait of Queen Elizabeth I, for whom Virginia is named. The portrait was a Christmas gift in 1926 to the Commonwealth from Viscountess Nancy Astor, a native Virginian who went to England and became the first woman to serve in the British Parliament. Her repartees with Winston Churchill are famous, and there was certainly no love lost between the two. Always remembering her Virginia roots as Nancy Witcher Langhorne, Lady Astor gave the Commonwealth the portrait of Queen Elizabeth I, writing in a letter her desire that the portrait be a reminder to the women of Virginia of the importance that women can "add to a country's greatness, even if they don't happen to be mothers!!" When our family arrived at the Governor's House the portrait was hanging in the north Ballroom.

Despite its known donor, however, there had always been questions about whether the portrait was a true portrait of the Queen. There were elements that supported its authenticity: it was oil on wood, not canvas, a style common during the 16th Century, and the dress she was wearing had elements of contemporary style, similar to known portraits of Elizabeth. However there were things about the portrait that made it suspect as an image of the Queen. The artist is unknown; her pose was extremely awkward, with the right arm foreshortened and at a strange angle; the background of the painting was dark and seemed out of context with the delicate features of the woman's face; and some of the clothing seemed to be over painted and perhaps added at a later date. But despite the question of its subject matter, the portrait was still a valued possession because of the importance of its donor. Along with the other paintings in the Governor's House which were suffering from years of exposure to cigarette smoke and uncontrolled temperatures, the portrait was sent off to be cleaned by conservator L. Cleo Mullins of the Richmond Conservation Studio.

The restored painting believed to be Queen Elizabeth I was perfect over the Hepplewhite bellflower sideboard in the Dining Room. Beneath is the coffee and tea service of the USS Battleship Virginia. Courtesy Library of Virginia

Art conservation is a painstaking, meticulous endeavor and the need for care is magnified on a piece like the Queen's portrait. Gentle removal of years of grime and layers of over-paint is done under special lighting under a magnifying glass. While removing the yellowed varnish on the portrait, small pieces of paint readily flaked off and Ms. Mullins realized that there was something beneath the top layer of paint.

Over paintings are not uncommon, and it began to appear that this portrait had something else beneath the visible picture. Often backgrounds of pictures are changed to keep up with fashion, or items are added or taken away depending on current beliefs, or damage is repaired.

Trying to determine what had happened to the painting over the years, Ms. Mullins had it x-rayed. Then infrared photography showed vague images beneath the surface. Yet despite believing there was an underpainting there, there was no way to know what would emerge if the paint were removed, or what the underlying condition would be. If the painting had been painted over because of damage, removing that paint might leave only the damaged surface below. There was also the chance that an insignificant image would emerge, rendering the painting basically worthless. It was daunting to have to decide whether to proceed or just maintain the painting in the form it had arrived in Virginia.

I made several visits to Ms. Mullins' studio to see the progress of the conservation and participated in the difficult decision about whether to proceed with the removal of paint to disclose what lay beneath the surface. Once the decision was made to go forward with the paint removal, our daring was rewarded and a fascinating series of images began to emerge. A third arm emerged, the original to the painting, which made the pose of the figure much more natural and evenly proportioned. Elements of dress that had been covered over by the floral background and chair reemerged and made the woman's figure much more delicate. But most significantly, a landscape background appeared which was quite in keeping with paintings of the 16th century. We had indeed ended up with a completely new portrait, but one which seemed even more likely to be a portrait of Queen Elizabeth I.

Despite these numerous new elements that emerged from the cleaning process, there was still no definitive answer to the identity of the lady in the portrait. Though it more than ever followed other known portraits of Elizabeth, nothing in the painting, including the still unknown building in the landscape background, connects the image with *absolute certainty* to Elizabeth I. Nonetheless, led by the words of Lady Astor, we hung the portrait in the most visible place in the Governor's House, at the end of the hall in the center of the Dining Room. With the planning already beginning for 2007, the 400th anniversary of the founding of Virginia, there was no question that the portrait, called a Queen Elizabeth portrait by Virginian Nancy Astor, would be the focal point of Duncan Lee's hallway vista.

But we wanted the other paintings in these rooms to be used to go further in telling the whole story of Virginia's significance in the history of America. Thus, in the place of honor, the center wall of the Dining Room, we placed the portrait of Queen Elizabeth, the virgin queen who oversaw much of the English age of exploration and for whom Virginia was named. In the north Ballroom we placed the portrait of Governor Alexander Spottswood, who as the leader of the Knights of the Golden Horseshoe opened Virginia to the west and the started the age of westward expansion. And in the south Ballroom, we placed the austere, often disregarded portrait of Nancy Astor, the native Virginian who became the first woman to serve in the British Parliament. I believed that with her accomplishments in life and her personal letter of encouragement to the women of Virginia, there was no one who represented Virginia's move into the modern world more than Lady Astor. With the placement of these portraits one could see the whole history of a state that, from its inception, was a leader to all.

Tracy Kamerer, Curator of the State Art Collection, summarized the Queen Elizabeth restoration project in an article in *Virginia Cavalcade*, Spring 2002. Ms. Kamerer worked diligently to ensure that not only the Queen Elizabeth portrait, but all of the paintings were properly cared for and documented.

"Bob Vila's Home Again." Continuing our efforts to share and record the work that was being done in the restoration of the Governor's House, we contacted Bob Vila, who was celebrating the 10th anniversary season of his television program, *Home Again*. We thought he might be interested in our project and consider doing a show that presented to his viewers our goal of making a historic home ready for modern living. Not only did Vila agree to make a program about the house, but he decided to make it the highlight of his Fall 1999 anniversary season and to film 13 episodes at various stages of the work. Each show focused on a particular element, varying from how we were conserving the historic parts of the house to the modernized features we were including in areas like the kitchens and baths. In addition to the television program, updates could be found on his website, BobVila.com. Vila was informed about the work's progress between programs by Sam Daniel and John Paul Hanbury so that plans could be made for taping to be done at appropriate points and so that there would be minimal impact by the production of the programs on our tight schedule.

In addition to the record that was made of some of the special projects we undertook, we were delighted that Vila decided to use part of each program to showcase other historic homes in Virginia. This was a wonderful way to spread the message about Virginia's heritage and let all of his viewers know that we invite everyone to visit our great Commonwealth. The anniversary series was shown in syndication for years afterwards, and I still have people from all over the country tell me that they saw it.

FROM LEFT: *Sam Daniel, Bob Vila and I discuss changes that would be made with the addition of a new wing on the northeast corner of the house.*

Courtesy DHR

The Support of Other Historic Homes. There is no question that there is collegiality of spirit among historic venues in Virginia. No other state can rival the number of sites important to the founding and growth of this nation, and Virginians have always proudly considered it their responsibility to maintain these sites for future generations. These sites work together to present properly conserved properties so that visitors can get an accurate understanding of life at various times in early Virginia. Because our resources for the Governor's House renovation were limited, I believed that understanding how other historic places had handled conservation issues at their properties would streamline our thinking about issues at the Governor's House and help save money without compromising quality. Sites that gave their support to us were numerous. The Valentine Museum, now the Valentine Richmond History Center, was one of the first sites where we sought help; The Valentine, led by Executive Director William Martin, was extremely important because its main focus, the home of John Wickham, was designed by Alexander Parris, the same architect who designed the Governor's House.

To our good fortune, Mount Vernon, the estate of George Washington on the Potomac River in Fairfax, was installing a new HVAC system as we were beginning to explore options for the Governor's House. Like the Wickham House, in that Mount Vernon is not used as a residence any longer; nonetheless, the HVAC system being installed at Mount Vernon did have importance for us in how their decisions were made about running duct work without losing important historic building fabric. Director Jim Reese arranged for me to examine the installation work in progress so that I could understand what was involved in this part of a project.

Perhaps the most engaged director of a historic Virginia home was Vernon Edenfield of Kenmore, the home of Mary Washington in Fredericksburg. Edenfield helped coordinate meetings and fabric selections with Scalamandre Corporation and his assistance with Scalamandre was particularly important in helping us keep our project on schedule. Edenfield also encouraged me to consider the offer of the Board of Visitors of Mary Washington College, now The University of Mary Washington, to display selections of their collection of works by artist Gari Melchers which were housed at his estate, Belmont, just outside of Fredericksburg. Belmont is currently maintained by The University of Mary Washington and we worked with their Board of Visitors and Historic Properties Committee in examining the paintings that would be used at the Governor's House.

Gari Melchers was one of Virginia's accomplished artists of the late 19th and early 20th centuries, and his home was being closed for renovations by Mary Washington at the time that we were reoccupying the Mansion at the conclusion of our project. Not only would we have some of the most wonderful art by a Virginia artist to adorn the newly renovated Governor's House, but we would also be helping The Belmont renovation team by caring for some of their pieces which otherwise might have gone into storage. In his letter to me, Richard B. Cooper, Chair of the Historic Properties Committee and member of the Mary Washington Board of Visitors, said "Many of these pieces are shared around the world in our American Embassies as part of the Arts in Embassies Program operated by the U.S. Department of State. With the re-opening of the Governor's Mansion and the celebration of the Mansion's history with Virginia arts, the Historic Properties Committee and the Board of Visitors would like to extend an invitation to you to share these paintings with the Gilmore family and the citizens of the Commonwealth." We gave Melcher's portrait of his wife, Corinne, one of their most treasured pieces, a special place in the Ladies' Parlor.

Notes

Chapter 1 – Alexander Parris Designs a Governor's House

1. Thomas Jefferson, *The Life and Selected Writings of Thomas Jefferson,* eds. Adrienne Koch and William Peden (New York: Random House, 1944), VIII Letters:414.
2. Jefferson, *Life and Selected Writings,* I Autobiography, 48.
3. Jefferson, *Life and Selected Writings,* VIII, 381.
4. Jefferson, *Life and Selected Writings,* VIII, 380–381.
5. Thomas Jefferson, *The Papers of Thomas Jefferson,* ed. Julian P. Boyd (Princeton: University Press, 1951), Vol.4, 225. The location of the house where Jefferson lived has not been precisely identified, but seems to have been in the vicinity of present day Governor and Broad Streets.
6. William Seale, *Virginia's Executive Mansion* (Richmond: Virginia State Library and Archives, 1988), 8.
7. Samuel Mordecai, *Virginia, especially Richmond, in By-Gone Days; with a Glance at the Present: Being Reminiscences of an Old Citizen,* 2nd ed. (Richmond: West and Johnston, 1860), 73.
8. Seale, 22–23.
9. Artifacts from the West Gate excavations are stored at the Department of Historic Resources. The photographic record is available on the Library of Virginia website at http://www.lva.virginia.gov/public/guides/mansionrenov/.
10. Journal of the House of Delegates, 1810–1811, 9.

11. Seale, 15.
12. Katherine Godwin, *Living in a Legacy: Virginia's Executive Mansion* (Richmond: Chamber of Commerce, 1977), 7.
13. William Moncure and A.B. Venable, *Memorandum of Agreement, March 1, 1811*, is found in Auditor of Public Accounts, Capitol Square Data, Records, 1776–1971, Box #3. The original is in the Executive Papers of James Monroe. Primary documents for Capitol Square data such as memoranda, vouchers, inventories, and reports to the legislature that are referenced in this work are preserved in the State government records collection in the Library of Virginia. Information in these sources is abundant for the 1800s, but Mansion documents become scarce by the end of the century.
14. Seale, 180–183.
15. Ibid., 183.
16. Edward F. Zimmer and Pamela J. Scott, "Alexander Parris, Benjamin Henry Latrobe, and the John Wickham House in Richmond, Virginia," *Journal of the Society of Architectural Historians, Vol. XLI,* 3 (October 1982), 202–211. We know that the house was altered from the original Parris sketch in various ways, perhaps after being reviewed by Benjamin Latrobe. Latrobe, the first fully trained architect to teach and work in America, known best for his completion of the United States Capitol, gave an unvarnished evaluation of the design Parris submitted to John Wickham for his private residence. In a March 16, 1811 letter to Wickham, Latrobe laments that he failed to see the plans before the project was underway. Latrobe said he could only comment "caveat stuccoator," his clear opinion as to a stucco exterior. Also in his analysis of the Wickham house, Latrobe opined that it was "inadvisable" to place chimneys where Parris had them, on exterior walls between windows and opposite doors; rather they should be moved to the interior walls of the house. In the only surviving Parris sketch of plans for the Governor's House, the same "faulty" chimney location is seen; the fireplaces are along the exterior walls of the house between windows. Since no such fireplace locations exist in the house as built, one wonders whether this change came about due to Parris' lesson from Latrobe on his Wickham house design.
17. Seale, 44.
18. James I. Robertson, Jr., *Stonewall Jackson: The Man, The Soldier, The Legend* (New York: Macmillan, 1997) 756.
19. Ibid., 758.
20. Seale, 120.
21. Ibid., 120.
22. Ibid., 120.
23. NOAA's National Weather Service internal data records can be requested at http://weather.gov/akq.

Chapter 2 – The Governor's House Changes with Time

1. Seale, 22.
2. Ibid., 125.
3. Ibid., 125.

Chapter 4 – Where We Started–Governor Tyler Would Have Felt at Home

1. Godwin, 69–70.

Chapter 5–Using Technology to Gather Historical Data

1. Seale, 19.
2. Etta Donnan Mann, *Four Years in the Governor's Mansion of Virginia 1910–1914* (Richmond: The Dietz Press, 1937), 218.

Chapter 6–The Hallway, a *Janus*

1. See photographs in Chapter 1.
2. Mann, 4.
3. Ibid., 3.
4. Ibid., 3.
5. Frank S. Welsh, *Microscopic Paint and Color Analysis* (Bryn Mawr, PA: Frank S. Welsh Company, 1998), 3. This document was the report issued by Frank Welsh, the architectural coatings consultant engaged to examine the original paint and wallpaper finishes in the first floor Front Hall, Old Governor's Office and Ladies' Parlor of the Governor's House. An initial effort was made in 1989 to investigate these finishes, but a more complete exploration was possible during the 1998 project.
6. Ibid., 3–5. One of the most frequently asked questions by visitors after the restoration was the shade of gray used throughout the first floor. The Munsell value for the walls was 5.7Y5.3/0.3. The paint used was Benjamin Moore 1473, lightened 25%. This shade of gray was used as the base color in the custom-made Gracie wallpaper in the Breakfast Room.
7. Many historic patterns for carpets, wallpaper, and fabrics are maintained by companies that specialize in the production of period furnishings. They are referred to as "documented" because they can be dated with certainty to specific years of production. Most purchases of these items must be through a custom order, and the production time for these custom orders is lengthy.
8. Seale, 127.

Chapter 7–The 1813 Rooms

1. Welsh, 3.
2. Catherine S. Myers, *Interim Report, fireplace Mantels, The Virginia Governor's Mansion* (Washington, DC: Myers Conservation, 1999), 1.
3. Other historic homes were always willing to give information and share ideas. Information about Mount Vernon can be found on their website, http://www.mountvernon.org/. Another most helpful venue was the Valentine/Wickham House, now the Richmond History Center at http://www.richmondhistorycenter.com/.

4. Information about the Gari Melchers House and Museum can be found at the website http://www.umw.edu/gari_melchers/.

Chapter 8–The Ballroom

1. The titles given for these paintings were those found on plates added to the frames at some after the paintings were finished. Frequently these plates contain mistakes, such as the attribution "St. James River," which was likely a mistake for "The James River."

Chapter 9 – The Dining Room and Breakfast Room

1. During our work, evidence of the Duncan Lee fireplace was found along the east wall of the Dining Room. A "ghost" of the mantel, about 7'11" wide by 5'8" tall, spanned between the two windows. An over mantel extended to about 9'10" above the floor, so the entire feature was intended to be an imposing element in the room and focal point of the long distance from the front door. In the few remaining pictures of it *in situ*, however, it is basically hidden behind the dining table and chairs. There was never any real consideration about returning the fireplace. It didn't have any history in the house, lasting less than 20 years. All of the reasons for its elimination still exist. As former Governors Montague, Byrd, and others opined, though the room is cavernous, there is no other long wall space in the room to place needed furniture. The New York Hepplewhite sideboard that is in the space now is one of the most valuable furnishings in the House, and there is no more appropriate place for such an exquisite piece than that wall. And then there were practical reasons - the chimney is no longer a working chimney and that would have presented huge issues.

Glossary

Architectural Terminology

Astragal	A molding composed of a half-round surface surrounded by two flat planes.
Balustrade	A rail and the row of balusters or posts that support it.
Capital	The top part of a pillar or column.
Chair rail	A molding used on an interior wall to prevent the backs of chairs from rubbing against plaster. Also called a dado rail.
Colonial Revival	A design movement in the United States between 1870 and 1920 (some say as late as the 1950s) which reused Colonial or Georgian designs.
Cornice	The uppermost section of moldings along the top of a wall or just below a roof.
Federal	A design period in the United States between 1780 and 1830 that blended the symmetry of the Georgian architecture of the colonial period with new styles of Neoclassical architecture in Britain.
Flemish Bond	A pattern of brickwork that uses alternating stretchers and headers in each course, each header placed actually over a stretcher.

Flute	Channel used to decorate columns or pilasters in classical architecture.
Frieze	A horizontal band that runs above doorways and windows or below the cornice. It may be decorated with designs or carvings.
Georgian	Architectural styles current between 1720 and 1840. In the colonies it became broadly known as Federal style.
Header	1- A floor or roof beam placed between two long beams. 2- A brick or stone laid at a right angle to the face of the wall so that only its short end is showing, Also called a bonder.
Jamb	A pair of vertical posts or pieces that together form the sides of a door, window frame, fireplace.
Joists	Small timbers or metal beams that are arranged parallel from wall to wall to support a floor or ceiling.
Lintel	The horizontal crosspiece over an opening as a door or window usually carrying the weight of the structure above it.
Marbleize	A form of faux finishing where paint is applied to create the appearance of marble. A technique to use economical materials to create the appearance of more expensive materials.
Mortise	A hole or recess cut, as in a piece of wood, to receive a projecting part (tenon).
Parapet	A low protective wall or railing along the edge of a raised structure such as a roof or balcony.
Parquet	A patterned, wood surface such as in a floor or panel sometimes with inlays of other woods or materials to create a design.
Pilaster	A rectangular support that resembles a flat column. It projects only slightly and has a base, a shaft and a capital. Used in Greek revival architecture, it can be plain or decorative.
Plinth	The block upon which the moldings of an architrave are placed. A square block serving as a base.
Pocket door	A door or pair of doors that slide into the wall.
Portico	A colonnade or covered ambulatory often at the entrance of a building
Tenon	A projection cut out on a piece of wood for insertion into a corresponding hole (mortise) in another piece to make a joint.

Wainscot	The lower part of an interior wall when it is finished in a material different from the upper part.

Furniture Terminology

Acanthus leaves	A *genus* of prickly herbs whose leaves are often represented in architecture, furniture and textiles.
Bellflower	A popular inlaid furniture decoration using the image of any of a variety of herbs of the genus *Campanula* that have showy, bell-shaped flowers.
Demilune	Crescent-shaped or like a half-moon.
Duncan Phyfe	A leading furniture maker of the 19th century who worked in both the Federal Sheraton style and the Empire Style; he frequently used curule or Roman style chair and settee bases, couches with scrolled ends; his motifs included reeds, lyres, swags, ribbons, and Acanthus leaves.
First Empire	Style of French décor and costume identified with the reign of Napoleon I. Traditional classical motifs are supplemented by symbols of grandeur, particularly the emperor's symbol, the bee, and military and Egyptian motifs. Not to be confused with the late 19th century Second Empire.
Hepplewhite	A cabinet and chair maker of the 18th century who made light, elegant furniture, including shield-back chairs.
Inlay	To set pieces, such as wood, into a surface usually at the same level, to form a design.
Ormolu	Finish used on metal to imitate gold.
Tester	A canopy, often used to describe a four-poster bed with a canopy.
Veneer	A thin, surface layer of a finely grained wood, glued to a base of inferior wood or other material.

Textile Terminology

Brussels Carpets	A loomed carpet made of colored, firmly textured, twisted woolen yarns fixed in a foundation web of strong linen thread; the woolen yarns are drawn up through the web in loops to form a pattern; the loops are not cut which makes the rugs very durable; generally used in high traffic areas.
Dimity	A sheer, usually corded cotton fabric of plain weave in checks or stripes.
Festoon	A decorative chain or strip hanging between two points.

Jacquard	A loom invented by Joseph Jacquard in 1801 that uses cards with punched holes in rows that each correspond to one row of a pattern design. There are multiple rows on each card and the cards are hung in order on the loom to control the fibers that are loaded in the appropriate order.
Oriental Carpets	Handmade carpets either knotted with pile or woven with pile usually with a highly stylized design; produced in the Middle East and Asia.
Taffeta	A crisp, plainly woven fabric made from silk or synthetic fibers.
Toile	A plain, simple twill weave fabric, *e.g.*, linen, particularly for painting on. Toile de Jouy usually has a white or off-white background with pastoral scene of a single color. Popular in 18th century France.
Wilton Carpets	A loomed carpet of similar materials and woven in a similar manner to Brussels Carpets; Wilton-style carpets differ from Brussels since their loops are cut which creates a velvety pile, generally considered more elegant, but less durable.

Bibliography

Primary sources for the Governor's House exist in a variety of forms. Vouchers, inventories, and reports to the General Assembly are maintained at the Library of Virginia. There is much information about work that was done to the house during the 19th century and what furnishings were there, but records become sparse by 1900. Governor's papers are held at various libraries, but references in these specifically to the Governor's House are scattered and difficult to find.

Findings made during the 1998-1999 restoration during the administration of Governor James Gilmore were photographed and documented by the Department of Historic Resources and are now maintained on the Library of Virginia Website. These findings form the basis for much of what is reported in this text.

Bell, John W. *Memoirs of Governor William Smith, of Virginia. The Political, Military and Personal History.* New York, NY: The Moss Engraving Company, 1891.

Boney, F. N. *John Letcher of Virginia, the Story of Virginia's Civil War Governor.* University, AL: University of Alabama Press, 1966.

Boyd, Julian. *The Papers of Thomas Jefferson.* Princeton, 1950.

Ferrell, Jr., Henry C. *Claude Swanson of Virginia: a Political Biography.* Lexington, KY: University Press of Kentucky, 1985.

Godwin, Katherine. *Living in a Legacy: Virginia's Executive Mansion.* Richmond, VA: Virginia State Chamber of Commerce, 1977.

Jefferson, Thomas. *The Life and Selected Writings of Thomas Jefferson.* Edited by Adrienne Koch, & William Peden. New York, NY: Random House, 1944.

Kimball, Fiske. *Thomas Jefferson Architect: Original Designs in the Coolidge Collection of the Massachussetts Historical Society.* With an Essay and Notes by Fiske Kimball. New Introduction by Frederick Doveton Nichols. New York: Da Capo Press, 1968.

Mann, Etta Donnan. *Four Years in the Governor's Mansion of Virginia 1910-1914.* Richmond, VA: The Dietz Press, 1937.

Mordecai, Samuel. *Richmond in By-Gone Days: Being Reminiscences of an Old Citizen.* 2nd edition. Richmond, VA: West & Johnson, 1860.

Robertson, James I. *Stonewall Jackson: The Man, The Soldier, The Legend.* New York, NY: Macmillan, 1997.

Seale, William. *Virginia's Executive Mansion A History of the Governor's House.* Richmond, VA: Virginia State Library, 1988.

Wise, Barton Haxall. *The Life of Henry A. Wise of Virginia, 1806-1876.* New York, NY: The Macmillan Company, 1899.

Index

A

Allen, Governor George 16,24,25,33,36,76
Alley, Gloria 28
Almond, Josephine 21,57,78,98,109
American Institute for Conservation of Historic and Artistic Works 60
Amherst County, VA 71
Architectural Digest 85
Arch of Sandstone on the Potomac River 72
Arnold, Kathryn 68,117,118
Ashland, VA 17
Astor, C. H., Nancy Viscountess 72,73,121,122
Austin Brockenbrough and Associates, L.L.P. 29

B

Bailey and Griffin 59,84
Baliles, Governor Gerald 19,24
Ballroom 10,16, 32,37,44,48-50,52,67-71,76,79,99,116, 120,122
Barbour, Governor James 5,15,16,63,65,66,131
Barboursville, VA 66

Battle, Governor John S. 77
Battleship silver 58
Battleship Virginia 59,78
Belmont 124
Beur, Christian 72
Bitter, Bob 62,117
Bitter, Mark 117
Blackhawk 65
Bliley, Rob 28,92
Brady, Matthew 19,20
Breakfast Room 16,24,34,76-80,82,95
Bridges, Charles 73
British House of Commons 73
British Parliament 122
Brockman, James S. 116
Broocke, Nathan "Irv" 25,27
Brooks, Bruce viii,27
Brunschwig and Fils 84,85,108,119
Bryant, Charles K. 18
Bryn Mawr, PA 42,113
Bulfinch, Charles 6
Byrd, Governor Harry 18, 19,46,48,72,75,104

C

Callahan, Jr., Vincent F. 27
Callahans Meadow, Virginia 72
Capitol Room 18,37,38,81,82,83,84
Capitol Square iv,v,1,2,3,11,12,23,28,33,37,38,80,82,83,89, 103,104,105,106,107,110,118
Carriage House 19,38,88,98,100,105,106
Carter and Company 119
Case, Donna 27,37,38,88,90,91,117
Cherwa-Ewing Engineering, P.C. 28
Churchill, Winston 121
Citizens Advisory Committee (CAC) 23,29,30,51,63,77,78
Civil War 6,19,24,69
Clagett, Mrs. Page B. 65
Clark, Jessica vi
Clérisseau, Charles Louis 1
Cochrane, Mr. and Mrs. J. Harwood 55
Colonial Williamsburg Drapery Studio ix,62,68,117,118
Connelly, Henry 55
Coolidge Collection at the Massachusetts Historical Society 2
Cooper, Richard B. 124
Copland, Charles 6
Corning Glass 58
Cornwell, Patricia 79
Cottage 4,5,38,89,100,104,105,106,107,108
Cowen, Greg 60
Crider, Jr., Henry T. viii,17,27,100
Crosby, William M. viii,27,29,100
Culinary Institute of America 91
Curtis, Mr. and Mrs. John 66

D

Dalton, Edwina "Eddy" 23
Dalton, Governor John 23
Daniel and Company 28,92
Daniel, Sam 28,90,110,123
Danville, VA 58
Daugherty, Greg 120
Davidson, A. 72
Department of General Services (DGS) viii,25,26,27,28, 29,30,39,100
Department of Historic Resources (DHR) viii,3,27,29,92-94,106,111
Deroche, Diane "Dee" viii
de Tessé, Madame La Comtesse 1
Dimmock, Charles 11,12
Dining Room 7,9-11,16-18,24,45,52,67,72,75-80,82,83, 95,98,99
Division of Engineering and Buildings 25,27
Drawing Room 7,9

Dressing Room 35,36,38,82,83,84
Duncan Phyfe 55,68,118

E

Ecker II, Fred 44,60,116
Edenfield, Vernon 117,124
England 52,60
Entry Hall 7,8,9
Everidge, Sarah vi
Executive Protection Unit (EPU) 30,33,34,37,39,45,81,88, 89,92,94,108

F

Fairfax, VA 30,124
Fairfax County, VA 72
Ferrell, Joseph 30
Finch, Amy vi,88
Flagler Museum ix
Forbes, Wm. 11
Ford, James Westhall 65
Fouquet, Jean-Pierre 1
Fredericksburg, VA 60,66,116,124

G

Garden Club of Virginia 109
General Assembly 16,24,48,78,81,103
General Assembly Building 28
George III 66
Gibson, Mrs. C. Huntley 66
Gillette, Charles 104,108
Gillette Garden 85,105,107,108
Gilmore, Ashton vi,32,108
Gilmore, Jay vi
Gilmore, Governor Jim 16,17,25,29,38,85
Gilmore, Roxane iii,iv
Gioia, John 30
Godwin, Jr., Governor Mills E. 15
Godwin, Katherine 23,112
Goodman, Paige 77
Governor's Palace 1
Gracie Company 77,79
Gray, Honorable and Mrs. Elmon 63
Gray Lumber Company 63
Gray, Peck 63
Gregory, John 15
Griffin, Jr., Anthony C. viii,27,104,107
Guard House 21,103,109
Gunn, James 73

H

Halpin, Mr. and Mrs. Gerald 72
Hanbury, Evans, Newill and Vlattas and Company (HENV) 28,68,85,117
Hanbury, John Paul 50,51,52,60,70,83,84,85,90,99,110,116,120,123
Harrison, Governor Albertis 58
Harrison Otis Gray House 6
Henry, Mrs. Leonard D. 66
Henry, Governor Patrick 15,64
Herndon, Chef Mark vi,27,34,90,91
Hight, Stacy vi,106
Hillwood Estate 68
Historic Properties Committee 124
Holton, Governor Linwood 29
Holton, Virginia Rogers "Jinks" 23
Horseshoe Farm 66
House of Delegates 27,111
Hubbard, Ruth 62,63,68,85,117,118,119

J

Jackson, General Thomas ""Stonewall" 12
Jackson, President Andrew 65
Jackson's River 72
"James River, Virginia 1860" 72
Jamestowne vii
Janus 50,54,55,67,113
Jefferson, Mary 2
Jefferson, Thomas iv,vi,vii,1,2,4,5,6,111
Johnson, David 72
J. R. Burroughs and Company 120

K

Kamerer, Tracy 64,122
Kaufman, Mr. and Mrs. George 68,118
Kenmore 55,124
Kenmore Foundation 117
Kennedy, Jacqueline 117
Kilpatrick, Kathryn viii
Kitchen 20,34,84,89,95,98,101
Knights of the Golden Horseshoe 73,122

L

L'Adeille et le Guirland" ("The Bee and the Garland.") 65
Ladies' Parlor 9,17,43,52,57,61,62,65,66,94,119,120,121
Lafayette 1,14,82
Lafayette Bedroom 14,18,35,82,83-85,86,93,94,119
Lahendro, Joseph D. viii,29
Lambert, III, Senator Benjamin J. 27

Latrobe, Benjamin 3,7,8,112
Laundry Room 33,89,95
Lee, Duncan 7,9,10,11,16,17,18,19,32,33,43,44,45,47,48,49,50,52,53,54,55,67,69,70,75,78,83,89,93,94,97,98,99,114,117,122,131
Lee House vi
Library of Virginia vii,ix,29,42,73,111,112,129
Long Island City, New York 117

M

Madison, James 2
Main Gate 110
Maison Carrée 1,2
Mann, Etta Donnan 11,49
Mann, Governor William Hodges 49
Martin, William J. ix,27,28
Mary Washington College 124
Matthews, Mr. and Mrs. Nick 55
McGuire, Mary Willing (Harrison) 66
McKim, Alexander 4
McPherson and Associates, P.C. 29
Mead, Peter 120
Mecklenburg County, VA 65
Medical College of Virginia 39,98
Melchers, Corinne 66,124
Melchers, Gari 66,124
Metropolitan Museum of Art 119
Metz, Cara viii,27,93,106
Metz, John D. viii
Miller, Mrs. H.C.L. 64
Mitchell, Jr., John F. viii,27,110
Moncure, William 4,112
Monroe, James 15,112
Montague, Betsie 17,48
Montague, Gay (Mrs. Charles Beatty Moore) v,12,13,48,63,64
Montague, Governor Andrew Jackson 12,13,17,18,21,33,47,48,58,60,61,64,75
Monticello vi,vii
Mordecai, Samuel 2,111
Moseley, Donald L. 27
Mount Vernon vi,vii,62,85,113,119,124
Mullins, L. Cleo 121
Myers, Cara viii
Myers, Catherine S. 60,113
Myers Conservation 60
Myers, John D. viii

N

National Park Service 49
National Weather Service 13,112

Index 135

New York City 119
Nimes, France 1
Norfolk, VA 28,68,118
Nuckols, Lewis 28

O

O'Ferrall, Governor Charles 47,58
O'Grady, Caitlyn viii
Old Finance Building 100
Old Governor's Office 17,43,45,55,57,58,59,61,62,63,65,
    66,92,118,119,120,121
Old State Finance Building 118
Oliver, Alex B. 30
Oliver Hill Building 118

P

Page, Barbara ix,59,68,85,117,118,119,120
Palm Beach, FL ix
Paris, France 1,2
Parris, Alexander vii,2,4,6-13,18,24,27,28,32,33,43-45,47,
    49-51,53-55,57,58,67,69,75,85,93,99,111,112,124,131
Petersburg, VA 63
Philadelphia, PA 55
Post, Marjorie Merriweather 68,118
Poston, William G. 27
Potomac River 124
Premier Millwork and Lumber Company of
    Virginia Beach 116
Prestwould 65
Prestwould Collection 67,117
Price, Governor James Hubert 18,69,76,98

Q

Queen Elizabeth I 73,76,121,122

R

Randolph-Macon College 120
Rapidan, VA 66
Rees, IV, James C. 62
Reid, Jr., L. William 27
Reminiscences of an Old Citizen 2
Restoration Committee 109
Richmond Conservation Studio 121
Rieley, William D., ASLA 109
Rixey, Mrs. John 66
Roanoke River 117
Robb, Governor Charles 18,24
Robb, Lynda 18,24
Robertson, Jr., James I. 112

Robertson, Wyndham 15
Robinson, Mrs. Francis Waring 6
Rockefeller Foundation 5
Rockland, MA 120
Rockville, VA 55
Roosevelt, President Theodore 8,9,16,17,48,61
Roxane's Lyre 62,63

S

Sadler and Whitehead, Architects, PLC viii,29,92
Sadler, Mary Harding viii,29
Sauers, Thomas vi
Scalamandre ix,55,62,63,67,85,101,117,124
Scalamandre, Flora 117
Scalamandre, Franco 117
Seale, William 111-113
Secretary of the Interior's Standards for the Treatment of
    Historic Properties vii
Shirley, Henry G. 27
Simpson, August Reinhardt ix
Slater, G. Bryan 25,26,61,109,110
Smit, Demerst B. 27
Smithfield, Virginia 64
Smith, Governor William "Extra Billy" 10-12,16,20,43,46,
    85,93,94,103,131
Smith, Russell 72
Spottswood, Governor Alexander 73,122
Stanley, Governor 20
State Art Collection 122
St. James River 72,114
Stourvale Mill 52,60,120
Stuart, Governor Henry Carter 8,17,18,21,24,75
Sulley, Thomas 66
Swann, Mary 66
Swanson, Governor Claude A. 17,48,49,75

T

Talley, Nancy St. Clair 109
Tam O'Shanter, 4
The Daughters of the American Revolution 64
The Foundation for the Preservation of the Executive
    Mansion 29,30
The University of Mary Washington 124
The University of Virginia 2
The Valentine Museum 124
The Virginia Constitution 15
Tidewater Preservation, Inc. 44,45,60,78,116
Times Dispatch 17
Tompkins, Christopher 4,43
Toombs, Bill 70
Toombs Electrical 70

Toombs, Mary Ellen 70
Townes, Martin "Tutti" 27,33,90,91,98,99
Trinkle, Governor Elbert Lee 61
Trinkle, Lee 37
Trinkle, Mrs. 37
Truman, President Harry 25
Tucker, Elaine Hamilton 117
Tuck, Governor William 76,98
Tyler, Governor John vi,4,31

U

US Centennial Exposition 48
USS Battleship Virginia 57,78,121
USS Richmond 78
USS Roanoke 78

V

Valentine Museum 27,42
Valentine Richmond History Center ix,27,113,124
Venable, A.B. 4,112
Vila, Bob 123
Virginia Cavalcade 122
Virginia Historical Society 66
Virginia State Library 111,130
Virginia Tourism Corporation 119
Volck, Frederick 12

W

Wallower, Mrs. Nancy Chapman 64,77
War of 1812 65
Washington and Lee University 55
Washington, D.C. 64,65
Washington, George 12,13,48,55,85,119,124
Washington, Martha 12
Washington, Mary 124
Watkins, Ronald M. 27,88
Waverly, VA 63
Weisiger, Minor viii
Welsh, Frank 42,50,52,53,59,60,113
Westcott, Michael 28
West Gate 100,106
Whirling Thunder 65
White Cloud 65
White House 16,25,67,68,75,117
Wickham House vi,ix,4,8,9,27,28,41,112,113,124
Wickham, John vi,4,27,124
Wilder, Governor Douglas 24,77,104
Williamsburg vii,1,4,5,15,85,94,118
Williams, Donald C. viii,25,27,29,110
Williams, Mr. John J. 71

Wilson, President Woodrow 78
Winchester, VA 24
Wise, Jr., H. Alexander 27
Woodward Grosvenor and Company, Ltd. 60,120
World Heritage List vii

Y

Yorktown, VA 55